Reclaiming the Merrimack

Reclaiming the Merrimack

An Action Plan to Clean the River

Dyke Hendrickson

America Through Time®
Adding Color to American History

America Through Time is an imprint of Fonthill Media LLC
www.through-time.com
office@through-time.com

Published by Arcadia Publishing by arrangement with Fonthill Media LLC
For all general information, please contact Arcadia Publishing:
Telephone: 843-853-2070
Fax: 843-853-0044
E-mail: sales@arcadiapublishing.com
For customer service and orders:
Toll-Free 1-888-313-2665

www.arcadiapublishing.com

First published 2023

ISBN 978-1-63499-479-8

Typeset in 10pt on13pt Sabon
Printed and bound in England

Foreword

In what might be called a "watershed moment" in the U.S. government's approach to clean water, federal legislation in 2023 is making billions of dollars available to communities along rivers that treat sewage and provide drinking water.

This is good news for hundreds of thousands of residents in the Merrimack River Valley. Communities including Manchester and Nashua, N.H., and Lowell, Lawrence, and Haverhill, Massachusetts, could benefit. All are under consent agreements with the Environmental Protection Agency to improve their sewage-treatment facilities, and this is a chance to do so.

Scores of smaller towns and cities on the river will also be better off because their sectors of the Merrimack will be more accessible for fishing, boating and even swimming. Close to 600,000 residents get their drinking water from the Merrimack. Their futures have just improved also. Not since the Clean Water Act of 1972 have river communities been in the position to benefit so significantly from federal aid to improve water quality. The federal Environmental Protection Agency (EPA) stated in late 2022:

> The nation has underinvested in water infrastructure for too long. Insufficient water infrastructure threatens America's security, and it risks people's health, jobs, peace of mind, and future prosperity.
>
> The Bipartisan Infrastructure Law delivers more than $50 billion to EPA to improve our nation's drinking water, wastewater, and stormwater infrastructure—the single largest investment in water that the federal government has ever made.[1]

Old-timers can remember when the Merrimack was a dirty, polluted waterway that adults tried to avoid, and kids were fearful of falling into. From 1820, when the first mill was constructed in Lowell, to the late twentieth century, factories, cities, and towns poured untreated or partially treated waste into the 117-mile-long Merrimack. In terms of geography, pollution started in Manchester, N.H., which once housed the Amoskeag Manufacturing Co., the largest textile mills in the country. Other major polluters have been Nashua, Lowell, Lawrence, and Haverhill. Many other towns, cities, and companies downriver added to the foul water.

The Merrimack River in Newburyport, with a bridge in the scenic distance. (*Dan Graovac photo*)

Much of a city's waste entered the river without adequate treatment. Also, surface water from heavy rain caring gasoline, pesticides, and street debris ran through old piping systems and into the river. Rural upriver New Hampshire communities were not greatly affected by the pollution. Big factory cities tried—with varying degrees of earnestness—to do better. Meanwhile, downriver municipalities like Newburyport, Salisbury, and Amesbury have lamented the downstream flow of waste because their beaches and riverside parks were tainted by numerous levels of pollution.

But after 1972, the Clean Water Act provided federal grants so underfunded cities could build better treatment plants. In 1987, the grants were replaced by low interest revolving loans administered by the states. Public officials had access to funding. The quality of the water improved. Newburyport became a tourist center, and each year, more than 1,500 pleasure boat owners rent slips or moorings. Salisbury has emerged as a mecca for campers who can visit the river one day and plunge into the ocean the next.

In Haverhill, Lawrence, and Lowell, residents returned to walking and riding along the river. Businesses in both states invested in new structures near the Merrimack. Still, in 2023, the Merrimack sometimes is getting dirtier, not cleaner. After heavy rains, combined sewer overflows (CSOs) result in millions of gallons of effluent flowing downriver.[2]

The EPA cannot stop it. This federal agency has the power to discipline the cities, but municipal officials in offending communities say they do not have the tax revenue

The basin of the Merrimack River, Newburyport, at dawn. (*Dan Graovac photo*)

to make major improvements. So, the EPA enters into a "consent" agreement in which municipalities vow to invest more money, but it a very slow, very complicated process.

Those days of frustration—and effluent—could be ending. This book focuses, in part, on the promising days ahead starting in 2023. If sewage-treatment officials in offending communities and in the private sector get energized, billions of dollars of improvements could be on the way. If the Merrimack could get cleaner, those who enjoy recreation on the river will be thrilled, and a cleaner waterway is another reason why those who drink the water can feel confident.

Reclaiming the Merrimack does not explain how forms should be filled out and by whom, but it does join other sources in informing people that there is money available with which to make improvements. It is not known how much a given community would receive. Much paperwork awaits those paid to work for a cleaner river. Yet this tome is announcing the time is now for seeking funding through the EPA and its associated low-interest Revolving Loan Fund. The book is also about the history of the river and the people who developed it, and it makes suggestions on how the river can be improved by individuals and local community groups.

I went to New Bern, N.C., in December 2022 to talk with activists who were responsible for winning the "River of the Year" award from a national nonprofit organization. They were honored with improving the quality of water in the 275-mile-long Neuse River. Also included here is a list and description of about seventy

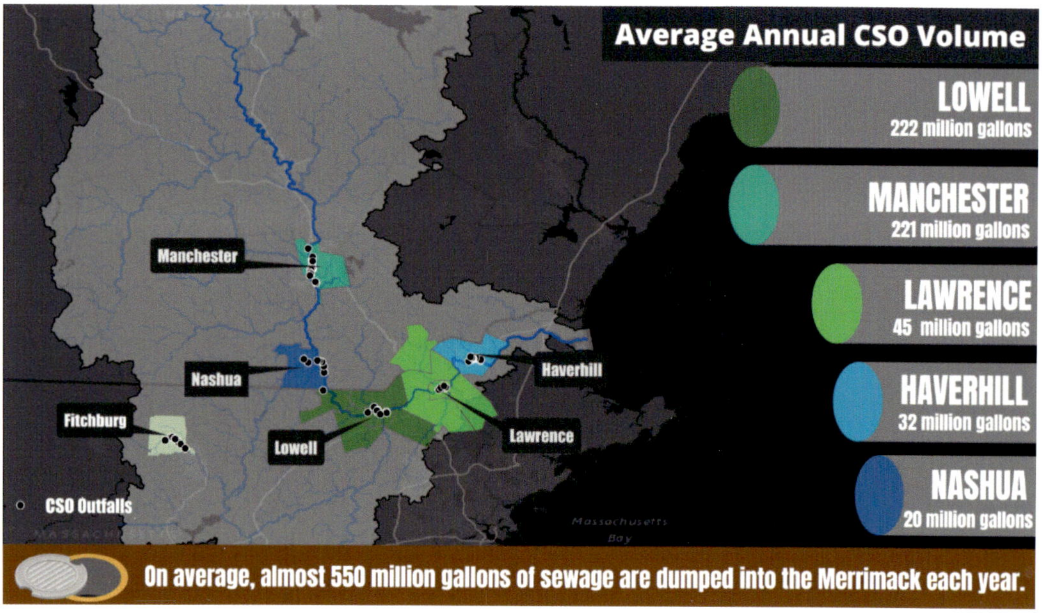

This map shows the amounts of effluent, produced by combined sewer overflows, that enter the river. (*Source: Merrimack River Watershed Council*)

tributaries to the Merrimack River. In order to have a cleaner river, we must protect the waterways that feed the Merrimack.

Now is the time to take advantage of a "second chance" to make improvements so the Merrimack also can be an environmental success story. If we are counting the Clean Water Act of 1972 as the start of this environmental process, we should realize that such opportunities come around only about twice a century.

Contents

Acknowledgments

This is my eighth book, and most have been made possible by generous supporters.

I want to acknowledge the Bowlen Foundation of Newburyport, which is supervised by lawyers James Connolly and Grace G. Connolly. This foundation has extended grants so this book could be written. The Bowlen Foundation has supported previous books: *Plum Island: A Vulnerable Gem* (2022); *Merrimack: The Resilient River* (2021); *New England Coast Guard Stories: Remarkable Mariners* (2020); and *Nautical Newburyport: A History of Captain, Clipper Ships and the Coast Guard* (2017).

I want to thank Dan Healey, after whom the Dan Healey River Education Program was created. He helps fund my research. Also, his program buys books about the river for teens and young adults. He wants more people in the Merrimack Valley to learn about the river—and what can be done to improve it.

I would like to thank photographers Dan Graovac and Bryan Eaton for contributing excellent photos. Dan had terrific shots of sunrises and sunsets. Bryan, for many years a gifted photographer for *The Daily News*, provided images that depict many facets of the river.

I want to thank Sharon Spieldenner of the Newburyport Public Library for helping me with computer issues, and John Macone of the Merrimack River Watershed Council, for enabling me to understand certain issues about the river.

My wife, Vicki Hendrickson, and our children, Leslie and Drew, have my gratitude for aiding me in the creation of this book and others.

Note: If a photo does not have a photo credit, it was likely taken by me—the full-time author, the part-time photographer.

1

The Concern of Thoreau and Good News for the Future

Naturalist Henry David Thoreau must have been one the most prescient Americans ever. In 1849, when he published the book *One Week on the Concord and Merrimack Rivers*, he remarked that the creation of several huge textile mills in Lowell was an idea that did not bode well for nature.

The growth of Lowell and other industrial cities on the Merrimack dramatically changed the river's ecosystem. Thoreau said one of the most noted changes was the disappearance of fish:

> Salmon, shad and Alewives were formerly abundant here ... until the dam ... and the factories at Lowell, put an end to their migrations hitherward.... Perchance, after a few thousands of years, if the fishes will be patient, and pass their summers elsewhere ... nature will have leveled ... the Lowell factories, and the Grass-ground River [will] run clear again.[1]

In addition to building dams, textile makers dumped wastes into the river. Federal historians say the canals of Lowell were especially loaded with trash and dyes, making the water unfit for drinking.

Population growth also contributed to the pollution of the water supply. By the 1870s, human waste and run-off had contaminated Lowell's wells, so the city began using filtered river water. Meanwhile, city sewage systems dumped wastes directly into the Merrimack. In the 1920s, 12 million gallons of Lowell sewage entered the river each day. Sometimes diseases traveled downstream from one river city to another, according to historians at the National Park Service.

There was no environmental movement two centuries ago. Indeed, community leaders in the nineteenth and early twentieth centuries did not energetically oppose fouling the river unless episodes of typhoid or cholera broke out.

The year 2023 marks two centuries of mills on the Merrimack River. The first mill was constructed in 1820, and the building continued until the end of the nineteenth century. Commerce in the riverside mills began diminishing in the 1950s. Now there are few active mills or shoe shops on the Merrimack, though the buildings and dams are still very visible.

Henry David Thoreau, who warned that riverside mills would ruin the purity of the river.

In the early 2020s, several dynamics are in action that suggest the Merrimack Valley is not living in the "roaring twenties" but the "revamping twenties." Rivers, lakes, wetlands, and oceans still are characterized by a variety of pollution. They must be cleaned, and help appears to be on the way. It is up to local governments and concerned citizens to act at this very important moment in time.

The Biden Administration has passed a $1.2 trillion spending package that promises to be the biggest clean-water spending initiative since the Clean Water Act of 1972. The Association of Metropolitan Water Agencies, a national trade organization, reports that the bill carries $48.4 billion over five years for drinking water and wastewater spending at EPA.

This massive infusion of money—and billions more from subsequent spending bills—is good news for riverside communities like Manchester and Nashua, N.H., and Lowell, Lawrence, and Haverhill, Massachusetts. They are communities that have trouble raising enough tax revenue to make major improvements to their waste-water treatment plants.

"This can be a great program for cities on the Merrimack," said David Cash, executive director of the New England bureau of the Environmental Protection Agency, during an interview on January 31, 2023:

> Recent spending bills say that close to half of the expenditure must go to cities with minority populations, black or brown residents. It is felt that less affluent communities are damaged by natural forces, like bad water and poor air quality.
>
> In the next couple years, a lot of funding is available for cities that want to improve sewage-treatment plants.[2]

An old riverside mill in Lawrence, topped by a clock tower.

For cities on the Merrimack, the funding infusion might be a case of poetic justice. In recent decades, such cities have had trouble generating enough property-tax revenue to develop aggressive improvement programs. Jobs have left the cities. New companies with potential might be reluctant to settle in riverside cities that sit on a dirty river.

Curiously, some cities that once thrived are now viewed as requiring more revenue to improve their own sewage-treatment operations. Haverhill, Lawrence, Lowell, Nashua, and Manchester are under "consent" agreements with the Environmental Protection Agency to improve their operations; these require the communities to spend more to improve their wastewater operations. The EPA will give them appropriate permits to keep discharging into the river as long as they continue to improve. But federal officials want them to spend more on improvement. Improvement—or at least discussion of it—is ongoing in those communities, but progress seems slow.

Residents in the Merrimack Valley Want Improvement

In recent years, scores of public meetings have taken place as residents, business leaders and government officials sought to identify the problem and come up with solutions. But the solutions are costly and complex. The causes of continued pollution include the following: combined sewer overflows (CSOs), loss of fields and forests, and the presence of "forever chemicals" that are not fully monitored. In addition, most riverside communities have pipes that let surface (rain) water into the river.

Some river veterans are patient. They say things are much improved from fifty years ago and are continuing to get better. Others, perhaps younger and downriver where the pollution congregates, are getting impatient. They say climate change is fostering more heavy rainstorms, and thus CSOs are continuing to foul the river. In 2021, a big year for releases, close to 800 million gallons of effluent entered the Merrimack, according to state officials. On bad days, feces can be seen floating in the beloved waterway.

In 2022, a Newburyport affinity group known as the Alliance of Climate and Environmental Stewards (ACES) released a poll that concluded 95 percent of respondents either were "very concerned" or "concerned" about the cleanliness of the Merrimack River. This high percentage suggests the health of the river has many adherents. But if this is so, why has it been so difficult to clean the 117-mile waterway?

CSOs (combined sewer overflows) are prevalent after heaving rainstorms. Bikes, needles, tires, and even automobiles are sometimes deposited into the Merrimack. Hundreds of pipes carrying dirty storm run-off head directly into the river. Also, construction, especially in southern New Hampshire, has been erasing valuable forests and fields.

It might be oversimplifying but here is what can be seen: Residents and clean-water officials of the Merrimack River Valley love the river but have not been fully effective in cleaning it. This book is about the history of the Merrimack, and some of its current problems. It is also a nod to a book that came out in late 2022: *Silent Spring Revolution Revisited: The Work of Rachel Carson, John F. Kennedy, Lyndon Johnson, and Richard Nixon.*

The author is Douglas Brinkley, an energetic historian who is one of the most prominent voices for clean water in the country. He says more should be done. Brinkley, as many others, notes that rivers, lakes, and oceans began getting cleaner following the Clean Water Act of 1972. Sen. Edmund Muskie of Maine was the key navigator of passage of that act, and I have included coverage of him in this volume. I knew Muskie when I was a cub reporter with the *Press Herald* in Portland, Maine, in the 1970s, and spent hours talking with him.

But Brinkley goes several steps further in his new book. He notes that Rachel Carson's *Silent Spring* (1962) helped start the Green Revolution. He also declares that JFK, LBJ, and even the rogue Richard Nixon played important roles in getting the movement started.

But so did Henry David Thoreau (1780–1852). He still casts a large shadow on environmental advancement. A favorite book of mine is his tome *A Week on the Concord and Merrimack Rivers*, written in 1839 and published in 1849. Thoreau noted that aggressive entrepreneurs building mills on the Merrimack in the 1820s were spreading doom for fish and other wildlife.

Discussions of "forever chemicals" that might be getting into the river suggest danger—if state officials had a clear understanding. Almost 600,000 people get their drinking water from the Merrimack. Communities getting their drinking water from the Merrimack include Andover, Methuen, Tewksbury, Lawrence, and Lowell, according to an EPA report in 2021. In mid-March 2023, the federal EPA announced it would be working to reduce these chemicals.

The drinking water in Flint, Michigan, was fine—until it was not.

Of course, the river in much of New Hampshire is clean. Near its start in Franklin, N.H., and going south, it is a popular destination for swimming, fishing, and boating. However, once the mills start in Manchester, N.H., the water gets increasingly impure.

The river starts in Franklin, N.H., shown here.

The Merrimack, north of Manchester, N.H., looks much like it did centuries ago.

Fishing is a popular sport near Salisbury, Mass.

The upper Merrimack, in New Hampshire, can be an idyllic spot.

Communities like Manchester, Nashua, Lawrence, Lowell, and Haverhill are still paying the price of a dirty and unregulated industry on their riverbanks. They do not seem to have enough money to make the necessary improvements in their systems. Communities downriver pay for their purported poverty.

On an institutional level, numerous organizations have been charged with the task of developing cleaner water, from the Merrimack River Watershed Council (Lawrence and Portsmouth) to the New England Interstate Water Pollution Control Commission (Lowell). The New England division of the EPA is supervising improvements. Communities on the Merrimack also employ their own wastewater-control teams.

Fred McNeill, a national leader in clean-water management, heads the Manchester, N.H., sewage-control operation. He says the Merrimack is cleaner now than it has been in many years. McNeill recalls that the Clean Water Act of 1972 provided billions for treatment plants that were constructed on the river's banks. Improvement started shortly thereafter. It is cleaner.

Still, effluent is discharged regularly into the river through CSOs. The old treatment plants were engineered so that domestic waste and surface water both enter the plants. In heavy, fast-moving storms, so much volume enters the plant that it cannot absorb it all. If it retained all incoming volume, the water/effluent would back up into homes and businesses causing significant damage. In 2021, a year with many rainstorms, close to 822 million gallons worth of CSOs were discharged into the waterway. With that the case, more CSOs are expected.[3]

Those who live near the river have different opinions on the threat of pollution. I went to a summer meeting of the Watershed Council in West Newbury, 2022, which was attended by numerous residents who own homes on the river. Some said they swam in the river during good weather; others said they would not dare to go in it. No one wants to eat the fish. After CSOs upstream are announced, almost all said they stay away from the water for several days.

When talking about the Merrimack River, there are at least two relevant sectors. Upriver of Manchester, N.H., the waterway is considered semi-pristine. Swimming is popular; the fishing is pretty good. But the waterway from Manchester to Newburyport is fraught with questions about its safety. When was the last heavy rain? How many treatment plants released CSOs? Is the river regularly tested for bacteria counts?

In recent years, then-state Sen. Diana DiZoglio, D-Methuen, convened numerous public meetings to discuss polluted water. These sessions were well-attended, with scores of stakeholders convening at sites like the Northern Essex Community College campus. Some were wastewater professionals. Others were city officials, taking in the dialogue perhaps with the hope of reporting back to concerned citizens, and there were homeowners who lived near the river. There is a lot of interest in cleaning the Merrimack.

The years surrounding 2020 seemed to be a "golden era" of citizen input on this subject. Wastewater treatment-managers showed up and were coaxed into explaining their challenges. Indeed, DiZoglio and others were able to unite many political figures. On Beacon Hill, legislation creating the Merrimack River District Commission was passed.

Some of the river's pollution comes from pipes like this, which dump foul surface water into the waterway.

Public Is Interested in a Cleaner River

One benefit of the commission's work is that that sewage-treatment plants now must announce when they have had a CSO and for how many hours. The administration of the program has taken some time to get started but it is a useful move forward. I have been observing clean-water activity since I wrote the book *Nautical Newburyport* in 2017. Here are some suggestions for a cleaner waterway:

Create a river czar. Right now, numerous commissions and boards are spread across Massachusetts and New Hampshire. One single individual with political clout and media savvy could help foster faster improvement. The federal EPA has authority over these two states, but many residents feel that it acts slowly in forcing improvements.

Hire riverkeepers. Numerous watershed areas in the U.S. employ staffers to monitor the river. Riverkeepers act when the public needs information. If there is a major CSO, riverkeepers would use the media and online postings to spread the word. If they are informed of an industrial dump into the river, they can check out the claim. If true, they can report it to the media and to government officials. A riverkeeper is part-scientist and part-activist.

Develop more institutional support. Environmental leaders should work to get businesses and universities more active in cleaning the river. When the Charles River was improved several decades ago, businesses and academic titans like MIT and Harvard helped force improvement.

Encourage more clean-ups. Though organizing a trash pick-up or a tree-planting day seems to be a small step, every effort helps. More schools should get outside in the spring to remove trash, and plant bushes and trees.

Launch more activism, develop more legislation. Environmentalists should keep the pressure on the EPA, which has responsibility for enforcing consent agreements. Residents should press elected officials to seek federal funding, which is now available.

File lawsuits. Citizens or environmental groups can bring lawsuits designed to force government and private industry to make improvements. Authors point out that the Clean Water Act of 1972 actually offers a clause that permits lawsuits against governments or private interests to help clean waterways.

A calm harbor can be a beautiful thing. (*Dan Graovac photo*)

2

A Coal-Fired Plant Still Operates on the Merrimack

Many residents do not know that a coal-fired power plant operates on the Merrimack River, in Bow, N.H. Activists claim that the water is heated before it is returned to the river, thus affecting the ecology of the waterway. Also, they say that managers have not installed a screening process that would prevent fish and other wildlife to be sucked into the plant. Here are excerpts from a New Hampshire Public Radio story in late 2022 by Mara Hoplamazian that highlight some of the issues.

A trial in a lawsuit against the only coal plant currently operating in New England began recently in federal court in Concord, N.H. The lawsuit, brought by the Sierra Club and the Conservation Law Foundation, is a citizen's enforcement case under the Clean Water Act, which turns fifty this week. Though laws and permits are usually enforced by the government, that act allows citizens to bring up a case in federal court to enforce standards that state or federal officials haven't.

In this case, the environmental groups say the coal plant has been breaking a permit by putting too much hot water into the Merrimack River, which harms fish and river ecology. They're asking a judge to determine that there have been permit violations and order the plant to rectify those and change operations going forward.

Lawyers for the plant say it hasn't violated the permit, based on current information and the steps it has taken to comply with a more recent permit that is not presently in effect.

"This is a case about the biological integrity of the Merrimack River," said Reed Super, a lawyer for the environmental groups, during his opening statement. The power plant has a cooling system to cool down steam that is used to generate electricity. The system draws up water from the Merrimack, puts waste heat into the water, and then returns hot water to the river. Heat is considered a pollutant under the Clean Water Act.

There are other cooling systems that can reduce the amount of heat that goes back into a water body, but the plant's owners have previously said an upgrade would cost millions of dollars. In his opening argument, Super said heat discharges can raise the temperature of a river out of an ideal range for the indigenous wildlife population and into a range more suitable for other species.

The number of commercial vessels on the river has diminished, but some fishing boats still go out.

Spring in New Hampshire means fast-moving water.

Under the plant's 1992 permit, it is not allowed to "change the balanced indigenous population" of the water it puts heat into. Super said the hot water is especially an issue when water levels are low in the river and the plant is operating at full capacity—a situation, he noted, that may become more common as climate change brings hotter and drier summers. Temperature data used by the environmental groups shows high temperatures have been an issue in the river as recently as this summer, Super said. The environmental groups are asking the judge to declare that there have been permit violations, order the plant owners to remediate the harm, pay civil penalties and do things differently going forward. Super said the plant should have to alert New England's electricity grid operator that it can't operate at full capacity when river flows are low or it should install a better cooling system.

Granite Shore Power owns the plant, which Eversource sold in 2018 as part of long-running efforts to decouple electric utilities and generation plants in New Hampshire. Wilbur Glahn, a lawyer for Granite Shore Power, said in his opening statement that the plant is operating within limits the Environmental Protection Agency has said are more stringent than the conditions of the 1992 permit at the heart of the case.

Lawyers for Granite Shore Power say they cooperated with the EPA to create the new permit and have operated under the limits set out in the 2020 permit since it was issued,

The state of New Hampshire offers numerous areas from which to launch a small vessel.

though they were not required to. Those limits, the defendants say, are stricter than the requirements of the 1992 permit.

Throughout his opening statement, Glahn focused on illustrating how much the plant has reduced operations in the past few years. Now, it runs as a "peaking" plant, burning coal to produce electricity only when demand is particularly high. The coal plant is committed to providing power for New England's regional grid operator through at least 2026. Because of their obligation to provide capacity for the grid, Glahn said the plant must "offer in" their power every day.

Glahn also suggested the environmental groups were using the lawsuit to try to shut down the plant and said the only way to reduce heat going into the river is for the plant to operate less, or not at all. It is not known when the case will be settled.

3

Survey Says People Want a Clean River

The Alliance of Climate and Environmental Stewards (ACES), an affinity group on the Merrimack Valley of Massachusetts and New Hampshire, has produced a three-year, two-phase opinion survey of Merrimack River "users" to determine how they feel about the health and condition of the river and organizers say the insights are disturbing.

In 2019, an initial pilot study—among the Merrimack River rowing community—indicated significant concerns about the health of the river. A Phase 2 survey, involving over 550 Merrimack River general users, was conducted in 2021 throughout the 117-mile watershed. The analysis of the data has been completed with survey responses indicating that 95 percent of river users are concerned to very concerned about the current and future condition of the Merrimack River.

And 73 percent of respondents believe it is unhealthy to be in the water of the Merrimack and to use it as a source for drinking water. Examining narrative comments submitted by the survey takers revealed that most of those non-suitability perceptions relate to concerns about combined sewer overflow releases experienced in the lower sections of the river. With significant governmental funds directed at health issues and communities focused on the environmental and economic health of the river, ACES provides this survey data to help inform the dialog and with the hope that it leads to a "River Rescue" movement.

Organizers believe it will need to involve a collaboration of all river-interested individual organizations, such as the Merrimack River Watershed Council and the Merrimack Conservation Partnership, as well as the Merrimack Valley Planning Commission and numerous NH and MA municipal, regional and federal political leaders.

The following ACES report provides data based on an analysis of the responses to the questions that were asked of the individual users.

Bridges must be built to last on the Merrimack. This photo was taken near Franklin, N.H.

Background

The Merrimack River provides a great recreational opportunity for hiking, fishing, boating, or sunning by the water. The 117-mile-long river drains a watershed of 5,000 sq. miles that sustains a population of over 2.5 million citizens, and provides major recreational opportunities. It offers diverse fish and wildlife habitat, and stunning beauty to more than 200 New Hampshire and Massachusetts communities.[1]

The river begins in the city of Franklin, New Hampshire, at the confluence of the Pemigewasset and Winnipesaukee rivers and flows south through Concord, Manchester, and Nashua. After entering Massachusetts, it turns east and north winding through towns and cities including Lowell, Lawrence, Haverhill, and Amesbury, to its mouth at the Gulf of Maine between the city of Newburyport and the town of Salisbury.

In this report, the reference to the upper and lower river is descriptive of the river from the source to the Lawrence dam and from this last dam on the river to the ocean. It is this free-flowing, ebb, slack and flood tides in the tidal zone that plays a large role in changing the use and interests regarding the river, and also the fisheries.

The Merrimack was once a pristine salmon and sturgeon river before being dammed and polluted in the 19th century Industrial Revolution, when several towns and cities on the Merrimack's banks (including Concord, Manchester, and Nashua in New Hampshire, and Lowell, Lawrence, and Haverhill in Massachusetts) took advantage of waterpower available from the river to build textile, paper and flour mills, tanneries, and even foundries along the riverbanks. The Merrimack not only provided power to

A quiet moment on a sandbar as the river approaches the Atlantic.

Colorful kayaks launch into the waterway.

these industries but also served as a means for the transportation of their manufactured goods.

Unfortunately, the river functioned as a sewer for industrial waste as well. During the peak of the textile mills, the color of the Merrimack River changed regularly depending on what materials were being dyed at the factories. Today, the Merrimack has been somewhat revitalized by the Clean Water Act of 1972 that mandated wastewater treatment plants, typically meeting water quality criteria for safe swimming and shell fishing.

However, on the rainiest days, surges of excess storm water flowing into antiquated sewer systems force the release of untreated sewage into the river. These events are called combined sewer overflows (CSOs). Because treatment plants cannot handle these larger surges of storm water, nearly 500 million gallons of polluted stormwater and sewage are dumped into the river during an average year. In 2021, a relatively wet year, the CSO release volume rose to 822 million gallons, the highest since 2013.

Despite significant improvements in environmental guidelines and supportive funding over the last half century, newer threats have emerged against the Merrimack: increased contaminated nonpoint source stormwater runoff; more frequent contamination from point source CSO releases; and the impacts from unsustainable development on land, forests, and critical habitats. Heavy rain events, which are expected to increase because of climate change, cause more water to flow off impermeable surfaces (roads and parking lots) picking up chemicals before entering drainages.

For the past four to five years, the Alliance of Climate and Environmental Stewards (ACES) has been supporting the importance of an ongoing broad-based, multi-state coalition that can raise community, state, and federal awareness of the urgency for a clean, safe Merrimack River. Because of public concern about the health of the river and its importance to communities in the river basin, water quality monitoring has been going on in the basin for years, but these programs have been sporadic at best and not coordinated basin-wide.

The lower Merrimack has emerged as a popular destination for power boats.

Above: A memorial for lost fishermen is a revered feature of the boardwalk in Newburyport.

Below: Creative statues dot the riverbank near Haverhill.

These programs make a good start, but larger coordinated multiyear data collection programs still need to be established. Since the citizens, towns and cities, and businesses are all potentially impacted by degrading conditions in the river, we all have the responsibility to change the course of events. But first we need an awareness of the urgency of the situation.

To this end, ACES has spent several years collecting anecdotal information to complement the physical and chemical data gathered by local, state, and federal organizations. This will provide a comprehensive user perception of the health of the Merrimack River. In 2019–2020, ACES conducted a pilot survey of 128 Master Level Rowers on the Merrimack. The results of that survey project are available on the website: aces-alliance. org/post/merrimack-river-study-rowing-community.

Then in 2021, ACES conducted a more comprehensive general users survey to engage a broader range of recreational and commercial users of the Merrimack River. These stakeholders, who regularly use the river, are crucial sources of information. This document summarizes some of the results of this survey. We hope this will provide authorities with information to help plan and fund necessary actions to make a healthier Merrimack.

We believe that the perspectives and experiences of the actual users of the river are critical for a more total understanding of the watershed's health.

Survey Responders

The survey targeted actual users of the Merrimack River from New Hampshire and Massachusetts. We did not ask responder's gender, race, age, or marital status. We only asked survey responders who are familiar with the river about their connections to the river and their opinions about the condition and health of the river.

We received responses from hundreds of people who care about the river, who use the river regularly, and who are concerned about the river's health. We found that 82 percent of our survey takers live in communities that border the Merrimack River and of those 94 percent live on or near the Merrimack and about 6 percent live on or near a tributary of the Merrimack. Most Massachusetts respondents, 78 percent, live from Haverhill downstream to the mouth of the Merrimack, where cumulative effects of all upstream pollution have their greatest impact.

Because this area is downstream of the last dam on the Merrimack River, many users not only enjoy direct contact with the water but also take advantage of the region's access to the ocean. Of those who responded to the survey, 69 percent use the river one or more times per week and 19 percent use the river once or twice a month.

Geographically, 81 percent of the survey responders' Merrimack River usage is in lower segments of the river, between Lawrence and the mouth of the river at Newburyport/Salisbury. The remaining 19 percent of responder river usage is in upper segments of the river between Lawrence and New Hampshire. Tributary usage (but not exclusive usage) ranges from between less than 1 percent up to 3 percent of total usage throughout the river basin.

Summarizing, if you use the Merrimack River upstream of Haverhill, you are much more likely to perceive no changes in the condition of the Merrimack River over the past few years. If you use the river downstream of Haverhill, you are much more likely

A small shed for visitors stands at the river's entrance on Plum Island.

to have seen significant changes in the conditions of the river. Perhaps this signals more CSO awareness. A majority of respondents believe the Lower River economy is highly dependent on three primary river related uses: tourism, fishing, and boating.

The Upper River economic dependence on the Merrimack is perceived to be more diverse, relying on tourism, fishing, water sports, rowing, and to a somewhat lesser extent boating. A majority (76 percent) of the 363 respondents indicated that they believe that there will be potential negative economic impacts as the river continues to deteriorate.

In addition, over 222 of those 363 concerned respondents registered their concerns by providing written descriptions and personal comments relating to those potential impacts. When asked what they believe to be urgent actions that need to be taken immediately to improve the Merrimack River, 84 percent of all survey takers put "Finding and fixing pollution hot spots and point source pollution" on their action list for protecting the health of the Merrimack River; 66 percent identified this as their highest priority for helping to improve the Merrimack River.

Their second most urgent action item (14 percent) was to "Develop an Alert System for combined sewer overflows." 93 percent of survey takers indicated that they agreed or strongly agreed that residents and users of the river resources should be given timely notification, information, level of risk, and possibly acceptable types of usage when sewage or potentially harmful material is released into the river.

Since this survey was conducted, initial actions have been taken to establish this type of a warning system.

The river can be rough, as this image suggests. The small house in Newburyport is a former clam shack. (*Bryan Eaton photo*)

Their third priority (at 11 percent) was to "improve habitat for fish and wildlife." Other choices like preparing for the next big flood, conserving water to mitigate drought, and promoting more recreational opportunities each came in equally at about 3 percent each.

Additionally, 230 survey takers responded when asked if they were aware that the Merrimack River is littered with both large and small forms of debris including cars, household appliances, plastic bottles, mattresses, tires, hypodermic needles, shoes, construction materials, bicycles, and furniture.

Over 90 percent of these respondents indicated they were aware of the problem and regarded this as a significant issue for the health of the river. They also believe that a portion of the funding from any future Combined Sewer Overflow (CSO) elimination programs should be allocated to cleaning debris from the Merrimack.

4

Study Shows Unsafe Bacteria Levels in Merrimack River

The following excerpt is from a story by Annie Ropeik of New Hampshire Public Radio in March 2022.

A new study released by the Merrimack River Watershed Council shows water conditions in the Merrimack River are safe most of the time, but on some days, swimmers and boaters may encounter unsafe levels of bacteria.

The council released the results of their 2021 water quality monitoring project this month. They measured a variety of water quality indicators along the river, including pH, salinity, and temperature. Volunteers also took samples of water to monitor the levels of two bacteria associated with fecal matter—E. coli and Enterococcus. For most of the samples taken throughout 2021, the levels of those bacteria were within safe levels designated by the Environmental Protection Agency, with about 20 percent of samples showing unsafe levels.

But for samples taken after combined sewer overflows when a mixture of stormwater, human waste, and other harmful substances is discharged after heavy precipitation by sewer systems that combine human waste, industrial wastewater, and rainwater runoff—more than half of the samples showed unsafe levels of bacteria. About 200 communities are in the watershed, with many using the river for recreation.

Combined sewers are an issue across the country, with almost 860 municipalities in the United States using a system that combines sewage and drainage into one pipe – a standard engineering practice throughout the late 1800s and early 1900s. When the pipe exceeds its capacity, such as during heavy rainfall, untreated wastewater can flow into a water body. Over 820 million gallons of combined sewer overflows were discharged into the Merrimack in 2021—the highest volume in a year since 2013, according to the Council. About 40 percent of the combined sewer overflows discharged into the Merrimack are coming from Manchester. Last fall, the city passed a bond resolution to address the overflows.

Nashua's wastewater system also discharges sewage into the Merrimack. Susie Bresney, a program manager with the council, presented the findings in a webinar. She said wastewater treatment plants are working hard to manage combined sewer overflows, but it's an expensive problem to solve.

Some dams in Lawrence are more than 100 years old.

"The problem is just so big that it requires federal funding to really solve," Bresney said during the presentation. "We're working on making sure that they have the funding available to really achieve the solutions that they need." The Council says they are also using the data presented in their report to better understand health risks associated with combined sewer overflow events and help municipalities implement green infrastructure. Bresney says that could help divert stormwater away from sewer systems, which make a big difference for combined sewer systems—which may be particularly vulnerable as New England's climate changes, becoming warmer and wetter, with increased instances of heavy precipitation.

5

The Big Picture as Seen by a Veteran Engineer

This article was written by Frederick McNeill, one of the most knowledgeable clean-water professionals in the region.[1]

For centuries the Merrimack River was the lifeline of the Indigenous peoples of northern New England, providing them food, clean water, and transportation. Many tribes including the Agawam, Amoskeag, Pawtucket, and Pennacook lived on its riverbanks. In fact, the name "Merrimack" is derived from the Indigenous American name meaning "swift water place." The first European to document the Merrimack River was the French explorer Samuel de Champlain in 1605. As more immigrants from Europe came to New England in the early 1700s, they settled along this river for the same reasons that the Indigenous people did—food, clean water, and transportation. Late in the 1700s, the lower Merrimack Valley transformed quickly from an agrarian society to an industrial society. The Merrimack River soon became a chief means of commerce and to this day has been the economic engine for the Merrimack Valley. This quest for commerce led to the river's pollution and near-death. Ironically, this same quest has also led to its cleanup and revitalization.

Industrial Revolution

The Pawtucket Falls in Lowell offered a source of waterpower that enabled the construction of sawmills and gristmills in the early 1700s. The Merrimack Valley's rich fields of timber gave local merchants a bountiful harvest. Transporting the timber down to the sawmills and the cities via the river, however, was problematic due to a series of waterfalls. In 1792, the Proprietors of Locks and Canals Association was established by timber merchants from Newburyport. In 1796, they built the Pawtucket Canal to bring timber products around the Pawtucket Falls.

This was followed in 1807 by the first lock and canal system in Manchester, N.H., which navigated around the Amoskeag Waterfalls. These locks and canals were built without any environmental awareness or consideration, and the Merrimack River was

Fred McNeill runs the treatment plant in Manchester, N.H. He is also a capable angler.

forever altered. In the early 1800s, at the dawn of the Industrial Revolution in England, textiles became one of the most dominant industries. The wealthy merchants on this side of the Atlantic, such as Francis Cabot Lowell and Benjamin Prichard, soon followed suit. The Merrimack Valley would transform over the next 100 years into a worldwide textile power led by the Amoskeag Mills, the world's largest single textile mill. The roaring flows of the mighty Merrimack River provided the power to drive this.

The river was literally the engine that drove the textile industry into prosperity, and the river into pollution. The wealthy industrialists with their growing textile industry continued to control the river's destiny as they harnessed its hydraulic power. Starting in 1820 and over the next twenty-eight years a series of dams were constructed on the river. In 1820, the Pawtucket Falls Dam was built in Lowell, providing 32 feet of hydraulic power in the form of hydraulic head. In 1836, the Amoskeag Falls Dam was constructed in Manchester providing 50 feet of hydraulic power. Last, in 1848, the Great Stone Dam was constructed in Lawrence providing 35 feet of hydraulic power.

In addition to these large-scale dams, canals were built in and around most mills, equipped with smaller dams with slide gates to control water release. Similar to the early locks, these dams and canals were constructed without environmental awareness or consideration. The slow killing of the Merrimack River continued. Huge textile mill complexes were constructed all along the riverbanks. From Franklin, New Hampshire, to Newburyport, Massachusetts, the Merrimack River powered the textile industry and New England's Industrial Revolution.

Sunset over the eastern portion of the Merrimack. (*Dan Graovac photo*)

Open water in Lawrence, with the youth boating club in the distance.

By 1840 Lowell had grown to thirty-two textile factories employing almost 8,000 workers. The world's largest single textile mill grew along the river at Manchester's Amoskeag Manufacturing Company, which operated from 1810 to 1935. During its peak it employed over 17,000 workers spread over forty buildings and 5.8 million square feet of flow space. The mills produced everything from military uniforms to the denim for Levi Strauss jeans. In addition to textiles, the company's foundries produced everything from guns to locomotives to fire engines. The mid-1800s represented the peak of the textile industry in New England and along the banks of the Merrimack River.

The harnessing of the mighty river was a civil engineering marvel for its time. Every inch of hydraulic power was used by these pioneers. Mill buildings were constructed to maximize water use. Massive turbines were constructed to harness the river's energy. Networks of canals and gates were constructed to distribute the water and its energy feature.

Clean Water Act of 1972 Was Crucial

The Merrimack River has been the center of life and commerce in New England since humans inhabited this land. It has also inspired generations who have seen and been touched by it. One of our country's first environmentalists, Henry David Thoreau, published *A Week on the Concord and Merrimack Rivers* in 1849, recounting his journey with his brother on this majestic waterway. Beatnik author and Lowell native, Jack Kerouac, reminisced about the river and its 1936 flood in his 1952 novel *Doctor Sax*. Several naval ships have been christened the USS *Merrimack* in honor of it.

This part of my article is about my journey as a forty-one-year water professional. I grew up about one mile from the site of the wastewater treatment plant that I presently manage on the banks of the Merrimack River. The Merrimack has inspired me since I saw its roaring rapids as a child. I have a lifetime of river memories, and I take great pride in now being a trusted steward of it. This article will look at many of the historical, social, and economic factors that contributed to the river's pollution, cleanup, and revitalization. This was truly a showplace of the golden age of civil engineering, constructed well before the birth of environmental engineering.

Consequences of the Industrial Revolution

The Industrial Revolution was driven in the name of commerce by a relatively few wealthy industrialists and merchants. They realized most of the financial and social benefits of their work, but the rest of the Merrimack Valley's residents suffered the consequences for decades to come. For centuries the river had been home to several species of diadromous fish that migrate between the ocean and freshwater. Shad, river herring, salmon, alewives, and eels served the river with several vital ecosystem functions throughout their life cycle. Diadromous fish transport nutrients from the ocean to inland ecosystems.

During spawning migrations, they also provide a seasonal abundance of food for species living year-round in marine, freshwater, and transitional habitats. Eagles,

Views of the Merrimack can be scenic from many locales, including this one in Amesbury. (*Bryan Eaton photo*)

The historic Lowell's Boat Shop in Amesbury still teaches youngsters the art of building—and navigating—wooden vessels. (*Dan Graovac photo*)

ospreys, otters, and many others rely on these diadromous fish to feed their young. Dam construction to fuel the Industrial Revolution all but killed the river's annual fish migration. The Great Stone Dam constructed just 30 miles from the Atlantic Ocean in Lawrence created almost a complete barrier for diadromous fish that had fed Indigenous peoples for centuries.

In addition to building dams, several "mill ponds" created stagnant water that further degraded the ecosystem supporting the river's aquatic life. While the altering of the Merrimack River's natural course harmed its biology, the mill pollution further deteriorated the river. Dyes and bleaches from the mills were discharged to the river daily. One of the most damaging pollutants was the "wash water" from cleaning equipment that contained oils, greases, and heavy metals. In addition to the textile mills, dozens of other industries such as foundries, tanneries, and paper mills contributed to the pollution.

In Concord, N.H., coal tar from the manufacture of coal gas to energize the city was stored in holding ponds within the river's floodplain. Population growth also contributed to the pollution. Mill workers had to live within walking distance of work, creating dense urban populations within the river's immediate watershed. Judicious wastewater collection and treatment was still decades in the future, and domestic waste was discharged directly to the river. Stormwater runoff that also discharged into the river carried everything from horse manure to mill tailings to slaughterhouse waste, further deteriorating water quality. The Merrimack River that had served generations of Indigenous peoples and early settlers became so polluted that it was an unsafe drinking water source.

Waterborne diseases such as cholera, gastroenteritis, and giardiasis traveled downstream from one river city to another. In 1832, a cholera outbreak in Manchester killed 674 residents. In 1849, 149 residents of Lowell died from the disease. The river no longer provided food, as the fish migrations had ended, and the water was so polluted that even boating on it was a serious health risk. The river had become so odorous in some areas that it was a hardship to live adjacent to it. The mighty river that had served generations was now almost dead.

The decline of the textile industry started shortly after the Civil War. The increased cost to ship cotton north, heat buildings, and pay workers contributed to the industry's demise along the Merrimack River. Most of the mills closed during the Great Depression. Urban populations deserted the cities for the suburbs. By 1940 the vacant mills represented a depressed era of inactivity. During this period our nation faced three great challenges that would take all its focus and resources: World War I, the Great Depression, and World War II. Although it was an acknowledged and growing problem, the state or federal government had done little to address the environmental degradation and water pollution. One of the first local laws to protect our waterways was enacted in 1878 when the Massachusetts General Court prohibited the discharge of refuse or any "polluting substances" into streams or public ponds. Commerce was again the priority, however, as lawmakers bowed to corporate pressure and exempted from this law the Connecticut and Merrimack rivers as well as the Concord River within Lowell.

In 1886, the Massachusetts Legislature required its board of health to adopt water pollution standards. This led to our engineering opening, with several notable activities taking place. In 1893, the Lawrence Experiment Station became home to groundbreaking wastewater engineering research.

Boats tied up at dusk can be found along the lower Merrimack. (*Dan Graovac photo*)

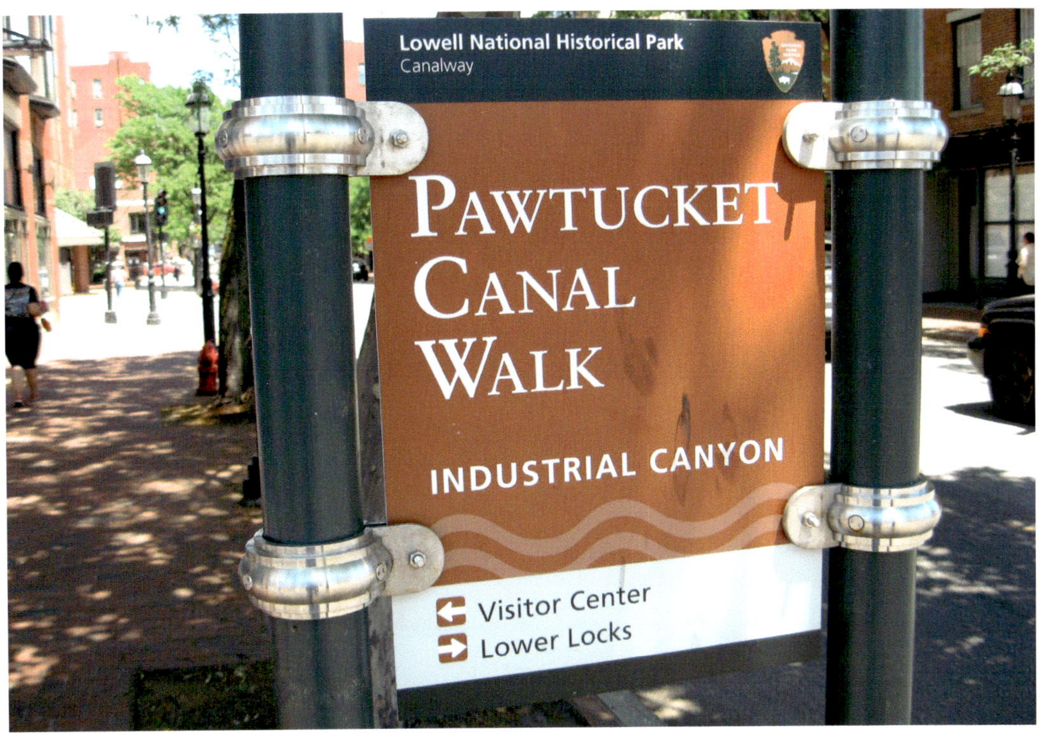

Lowell offers one of the most educational parks in the country relating to the old days on the river.

In 1899, the Rivers and Harbors Appropriation Act was passed, arguably our country's first federal environmental law. Ironically, this act addressed navigation of harbors but not the water quality. Once again, the law was driven by commerce; our harbors and adjacent waterways had become so full of solid waste that ships carrying goods could not navigate them. In 1912, the federal government passed the Public Health Service Act to study problems of sanitation, sewage, and pollution. In 1917, Lowell prepared an engineering report recommending "the construction of proper sewerage facilities" along the Merrimack River. In 1929, our organization, NEWEA, was founded as the New England Sewage Works Association with forty charter members.

Environmental awareness was increasing, and small but positive steps were addressing the pollution of the Merrimack River. With the end of World War II our nation could turn its attention to other challenges, including water pollution. In 1945, the surgeon general warned that over half of the U.S. population relied on drinking water supplies of "doubtful purity." In 1947, the New England Interstate Water Pollution Control Commission was created—one of several interstate water pollution control commissions created by Congress to address water pollution at the state level. By now the post-World War II generation recognized that water pollution was a national problem, and in 1948, the Federal Water Pollution Control Act was enacted. Although initially a weak law with no funding and little leadership, it was the foundation of the legislation that would ultimately enable the cleaning of the United States' waterways.

The Federal Water Pollution Control Act was amended in 1956, 1961, 1965, and 1966, and each time it became stronger and more sustainable. Meanwhile, along the Merrimack River the Anadromous Fish Conservation Act of 1965—a joint state–federal effort to restore migratory fish such as salmon and shad—was enacted. Fish ladders and elevators were constructed around dams to facilitate the migration of these fish. Recognition of a major problem was slowly being made. As a result of decades of inaction and continued raw wastewater discharges, the Merrimack River was named one of the 10 most polluted rivers in the country in the late '60s. However, the 1960s also brought change to our country. Social activism was bringing an end to an unpopular war in Vietnam. This same spirit of social activism embraced the environment.

Kayakers near Haverhill on a warm sunny day. (*Dan Graovac photo*)

In 1970, the first Earth Day was held in support of the environment. The Nashua River, a tributary of the Merrimack River, was severely polluted. Also in 1970, EPA was created and at last the United States' environmental leadership void began to be filled. Soon after, in the same year, the Clean Air Act was passed to address the smog choking our cities. Next up was water. One of New England's own, Sen. Edmund S. Muskie of Maine, championed clean water in the 1960s. Muskie grew up in Rumford, Maine, near the Androscoggin River, which received pollutants from paper mills, municipal sewers, and agricultural runoff. He knew firsthand that our nation's rivers were dying. In 1972, the U.S. House and Senate voted nearly unanimously to pass a set of sweeping amendments to the 1948 Federal Water Pollution Control Act. President Richard Nixon, however, vetoed the bill. The Muskie-led environmental coalition quickly secured the votes for an override by the Senate and House, and the bill became law on October 17, 1972. The newly amended Federal Water Pollution Control Act, now strengthened, funded, and provided leadership by the EPA, would be known as the Clean Water Act (CWA).

The CWA established environmental stewardship as one of our nation's priorities. It was also the catalyst for one of the most significant and successful engineering achievements over the past 100 years, the cleaning of our nation's waterways that had been polluted for over 200 years. The CWA established two key regulations to govern and protect our rivers: permits and water quality standards. The most important permit created was the National Pollutant Discharge Elimination System (NPDES), which regulates point sources discharging pollutants into U.S. waters.

Water quality standards were generally left to the states because of the geographical, climatic, and aquatic life variations among them. These numerical criteria provided clear guidance to our industry for meeting the CWA's goals. Most important to the CWA was federal funding. Many previous water projects suffered from lack of funding and lack of financial responsibility for the polluting industries. The CWA provided federal funding for construction of wastewater treatment plants WWTPs and collection systems nationwide, with the funding sources established at 90 percent federal, 5 percent state, and 5 percent local.

With the water quality standards, permits, and funding in place, our industry was ready to go to work.

Fishing on the jetties adjacent to the Merrimack brings many anglers. (*Bryan Eaton photo*)

Success of the Clean Water Act

The Merrimack River communities began the construction of nine WWTPs, starting at the river's confluence in Franklin and ending at its discharge in Newburyport. These nine WWTPs were the most cost-effective investment to address the polluted waters of the Merrimack River.

As treatment plants started up in the mid-1970s, river water quality improved immediately. As our nation embraced environmental stewardship, EPA determined that WWTPs were only a partial solution. Therefore, over the next thirty years, EPA established several other programs under the CWA that further improved water quality. In 1981, the Industrial Pretreatment Program was established to prevent the introduction of pollutants to a WWTP.

In 1990, the Municipal Separate Storm Sewer System (MS4) stormwater permit was issued to address polluted runoff affecting waterways. In 1994, EPA issued its Combined Sewer Overflow (CSO) Control Policy. This policy greatly affected the Merrimack River, as five large communities had combined sewer plants. That included Manchester, Nashua, Lowell, Lawrence and Haverhill. These communities each established long-term control plans to mitigate CSO discharges, and collectively they have invested over $1 billion in addressing CSOs. As a result, "separated" collection systems now flow to WWTPs. In the 2000s, EPA continued to improve water quality through NPDES permits by regulating dissolved pollutants such as nutrients including nitrogen and phosphorus. This multi-phase water pollution abatement approach over the past fifty years has restored the health and well-being of the Merrimack River, which is now the cleanest and healthiest it has been in almost 200 years.

The river is the second largest surface drinking water source in New England, serving 600,000 people through five water treatment plants. Manchester is constructing its new $40 million water treatment plant on the banks of the Merrimack River. The reclaimed river has once again become the economic engine of the Merrimack Valley, but this time sustainably so.

The river is still used to power our industries, but in a more environmentally responsible manner. Eight dams along the Merrimack furnish over 264,000 gallons per second of flow to turbines creating power in accordance with today's rules and regulations. The textile mill buildings along the river's banks are again thriving with high-tech companies, schools, and offices of several engineering firms contributing to our industry. While our nation's thirst for commerce and wealth has not subsided, we have recognized that this pursuit must be done environmentally, responsibly, and sustainably for our health and well-being.

In my youth I was in awe of the mighty Merrimack River with its white-water rapids and raw power as it roared during spring snowmelt and rains. I fished the river and witnessed firsthand the pollution and devastation done to this great waterway. During the winters in the 1960s I watched city trucks dump, as was standard practice, all the snow full of roadway contaminants and solid waste into the river through the bridge grating. In my lifetime the river has gone from unsightly, not swimmable, and unsuitable for aquatic life to its cleanest and healthiest state in almost 200 years. Full recreational activities are offered on the northern portion, including swimming, boating, water skiing, and fishing. Salmon are stocked annually in the upper reaches. Many of the

The number of pleasure boats has increased in recent years.

Close to 600,000 residents get their drinking water from the Merrimack. (*Dan Graovac photo*)

aquatic species that disappeared during the industrial revolution have slowly returned to their natural habitat. The river has once again become an inspiration to me and, I hope, to our next generations of environmentalists. The CWA was critical in achieving one of our nation's greatest engineering achievements in the past 100 years: the cleaning of the Merrimack River and the United States' waterways.

About the Author: Frederick McNeill is the chief engineer of Manchester, New Hampshire's Environmental Protection Division, where he manages northern New England's largest wastewater utility. In addition to his current role as NEWEA president, McNeill is a member of the New Hampshire Rivers Management Advisory Committee and has been a NEIWPCC commissioner since 2007. A longtime industry advocate, McNeill has published/ presented over 50 technical papers on a wide range of environmental engineering topics. He began his career as a Peace Corps volunteer managing a rural water supply program in Sierra Leone, West Africa. He then embarked on a 20-year stint as an engineering consultant, spending considerable time in Egypt, Jordan, Armenia, Georgia, and Bulgaria. In 2006, McNeill assumed his current position, chief engineer for the City of Manchester's Environmental Protection Division, where he manages northern New England's largest wastewater utility. He is the state director for the New England Water Environment Association and a member of the New Hampshire Rivers Management Advisory Committee. McNeill has a master's in business administration from Southern New Hampshire University and a bachelor's in civil engineering from Northeastern University.[2]

6

History of the Clean Water Act of 1972

This summary is excerpted from a paper by Environmental Works, a nonprofit research center in Seattle. The Clean Water Act has been the most important environmental legislation in the past century. Old-timers and young people alike who value the Merrimack River say that this legislation saved the waterway. But it took a long time for lawmakers to pass regulations that would cut down on pollution.

Our nation's commitment to protect the chemical, physical, and biological integrity of our waters began in 1899 with the River and Harbors Act. Improvement continued in 1948 with the establishment of the Federal Pollution Control Act and then transformed into the Clean Water Act in the 1970s. In the past few decades, the Clean Water Act has improved the health of rivers, lakes, and coastal waters throughout the United States. Here is a brief history of the Clean Water Act.

1948

The history of the Clean Water Act begins with its predecessor, the Federal Water Pollution Control Act of 1948, which was the first major law to address water pollution in the United States. Administered by the Environmental Protection Agency (EPA), this law created a set of comprehensive water quality programs and provided some financing to state and local governments.

1972

In the years following the introduction of the Federal Water Pollution Control Act, the American public became more concerned about controlling water pollution. In the early 1970s, two-thirds of the nation's lakes, rivers, and coastal waters were unsafe for fishing or swimming, and untreated sewage was dumped into open water. Extensive, wide-ranging amendments to the Federal Water Pollution Act occurred in 1972, and

Sunsets can make a good day even better. (*Dan Graovac photo*)

because the law had changed so drastically, its name soon shifted as well. It became commonly known by the name that endures to this day, the Clean Water Act. The 1972 amendments accomplished all of the following:

Established a system to regulate pollutant discharges into the waters of the U.S.
Granted the EPA the authority to implement pollution control programs.
Retained existing requirements to set water quality standards for all contaminants in surface waters.
Prohibited the discharge of a pollutant from a point source into navigable waters unless the person obtains a permit under the law's provisions.
Funded the construction of sewage treatment plants.
Recognized the importance of planning when tackling critical issues caused by non-point source pollution.

The 1980s

In the 1980s, the law was modified further. The EPA made the municipal construction grants process more efficient in 1981, which assisted treatment plans built under the program. A few years later, in 1987, the EPA phased out the construction grants program and replaced it with the Clean Water State Revolving Fund, which developed existing EPA-state partnerships to address water quality issues. Sen. George Mitchell of Maine was instrumental in achieving a compromise with the Reagan Administration so local communities would have access to federal loan money.

Recent Years

In the past few years, the definition of "waters of the United States," a critical term used in the Clean Water Act, has been up for debate. From the 1970s to the 1990s, most federal courts and agencies interpreted a broad scope of jurisdiction for the Clean Water Act. In the early 2000s, the Supreme Court held that the scope must be interpreted more narrowly, and in 2015, the EPA released a rule on the definition, but this was met with opposition. The Biden Administration is expanding the role of regulators, and it appears more streams, rivers and wetlands will be protected in the future.

7
The Modern Role of the EPA in New England

The New England division of the Environmental Protection Agency is a major force in the effort to clean the Merrimack. It is among the most powerful organizations in the region when it comes to requiring communities and industries to follow the rules. It is a Boston-based organization with many capable scientists developing data that will ostensibly help the waterway. Career professionals are trying to come up with solutions to vexing problems, such as how can we stop CSOs from fouling the river during the increasing number of heavy rainstorms.

The regional EPA has been working with Merrimack River stakeholders for decades. EPA staffers themselves can appear elusive, to wit, they do not seem to reach out to the people to hear the concerns of those who dwell near the river. Still, EPA managers have fostered improvements, and from their documents, below, they have useful goals. Most information here comes from the EPA website. This is an unsigned essay by the Environmental Protection Agency referencing the regional EPA's work with the Merrimack River.—DCH

Merrimack River Watershed

Goal: To improve Merrimack River water quality and make it safer for residents to use and enjoy the river for recreation.

Results: Federal, state and local governments, non-profit groups and concerned citizens are working together on a comprehensive strategy to improve water quality on the Merrimack River. The strategy addresses risks from litter, severe flooding and poor water quality.

Project Details: Contamination on the Merrimack comes from many sources including litter, stormwater runoff, combined sewer overflows (CSOs) and sewage leaking from old water infrastructure. EPA has worked with many government and non-government partners to implement strategies to improve Merrimack River water quality. EPA is supporting efforts to improve Merrimack water quality through stakeholder engagement, training, educational support, funding, and regulatory enforcement.

Training and Educational Support: EPA has helped Merrimack communities develop response plans to address risks from accidental spills of oil or chemicals at nearby plants. This support has included mapping, training, and tabletop exercises to improve preparedness and response capabilities that threaten the river. Educational support from EPA has provided funding and expertise to support "Water Boot Camps," to encourage high school students to pursue future careers in the water industry.

Funding: EPA provides critical funding through the State Revolving Fund, which has spurred important upgrades to the Greater Lawrence Sanitary District, the wastewater treatment plant that discharges to the Merrimack. The plant can now accept liquid food waste and has a robust combined heat and power system so the district can run its own operations if it loses electricity. The backup power prevents raw sewage from discharging into the Merrimack during an outage. The plant also converts food waste into gas which helps reduce the total cost of its energy greenhouse gas emissions.

Enforcement: EPA has issued Clean Water Act actions that require communities to remove illicit connections of sewers to storm drains. Five communities have been ordered by EPA to replace combined sewers that discharge untreated sewage during wet weather and make other major infrastructure improvements. For example, a significant regulatory enforcement action was settled in August 2020 with the City of Manchester which includes a plan to significantly reduce CSO overflows into the Merrimack River. At a cost of $231 million, the city will reduce CSOs to the river by over 50 percent,

The fast-running Merrimack, shown here in Manchester, N.H., was the key to hydropower for textile mills.

from 280 to 73 million gallons per year. To accomplish this, Manchester will disconnect streams from its sewer system by building a 2.5-mile culvert under the downtown area and installing separate storm sewers. Because of the significant public interest in overflows, the consent decree requires Manchester to monitor discharge flow from its CSO outfalls and notify the public within twenty-four hours on its website.

Ongoing Challenges: The Merrimack River continues to receive bacteria when rainstorms overwhelm the sewer system, and six communities together discharge hundreds of millions of gallons of untreated sewage in a typical year. The river is also contaminated by stormwater runoff and illicit sewage discharges into storm drains. The blue-green algae blooms from excess nutrients flowing into the river indicate the river is stressed. Between 2015 and 2019 EPA collected data from two real-time water monitors to help us understand some of the challenges facing those communities. EPA has published a summary report of its efforts on Merrimack River projects.

And it notes: A local nonprofit has hauled out more than 100,000 tons of garbage, including seventy-three cars and more than 8,000 tires, in the last thirteen years. More recently large numbers of hypodermic needles left by illegal drug users have been found floating in some portions of the river, causing major water quality problems.[1]

8

Sen. Edmund S. Muskie, Architect of Clean Water Act

Edmund S. Muskie grew up in Rumford, Maine, near the Androscoggin River, which received pollutants from paper mills and municipal sewage as well as sources like agricultural and street runoff. The geographic and geologic attributes of the Androscoggin, like other rivers in Maine and elsewhere, made it ideal for industry and pollution. He was a graduate of Bates College, in Lewiston, Maine.[1]

The Androscoggin River, from its source in the Rangeley Lakes to its outlet in Merrymeeting Bay, drops 1,500 vertical feet. Those drops, often in scenic falls, such as Great Falls in Lewiston-Auburn painted by Josiah Spooner Swift in 1830, are excellent sources of waterpower, and drew industry to the rivers' shores beginning in the early nineteenth century—and settlements, which also brought sources of pollution, even earlier.

Before Edmund S. Muskie went to the U.S. Senate in 1959, the problems of the Androscoggin River had come to the fore through the work of Dr. Walter Lawrance, a Bates College chemistry professor. Since the 1880s when paper mills began creating pulp with a sulfite chemical process, water downstream of paper mills often smelled awful and was too polluted to use. A study of the Androscoggin in the early 1940s showed that it had almost no dissolved oxygen and therefore could not support fish or aquatic life. Lawrance was named Androscoggin River Master in 1948 and, a year later, was given the authority by the state to set discharge limits. The river was threatened not only by industrial chemicals, but also by organic debris from log drives and by agricultural and sewage runoff. Lawrance's limits on industrial discharge led to changes in the way paper mills processed pulp. He also introduced sodium nitrate into the river to improve its oxygen levels and hence its odor and the health of the river. While Walter Lawrance worked to improve the water quality of the Androscoggin River, Muskie operated on a larger stage.

When he was elected to the U.S. Senate in 1958, he was assigned to the Public Works Committee, which had little influence. Now known as the father of the modern environmental movement, Muskie turned the committee and its Subcommittee on Air and Water Pollution, formed in 1965, into important voices. Muskie believed that

Above: Summer at Plum Island can be a memorable season. (*Courtesy photo*)

Below: Former Sen. Edmund S. Muskie, a graduate of Bates College, was a strong advocate of clean water. (*Bates College Archive*)

environmental regulations needed enough science and scientific analysis to justify the Federal government getting involved. Muskie and the committee wanted the Public Health Service, which had a charge to deal with pollution, to collect scientific evidence of the effects of pollution on health and welfare. Leon G. Billings, the former staffer of the Air and Water Pollution subcommittee, wrote, "Better science argues for more, rather than less, aggressive pollution controls."

Muskie was known for thoroughly studying issues and basing his arguments for legislation on the facts he gathered. Muskie shepherded the 1963 Clean Air Act through Congress and stood close to President Lyndon Johnson as he signed the landmark law. Muskie later said his greatest achievement was the 1970 Clean Air Act, an act that led the way to the 1972 clean water bill. As a number of Muskie's assistants and colleagues from the 1960s note, "environmental" was not a term much used then. There was a conservation movement that focused on preserving wild lands. Muskie's focus was different—he wanted to clean up the air, water, and land. When the polluted Cuyahoga River in Cleveland caught fire in 1969, Muskie's crusade for clean water drew a larger audience.

Muskie's reputation as a steward of the environment earned him the nickname "Mr. Clean" and drew letters from people around the country seeking his intervention or support for clean air and clean water causes. Suzanne Clune, an eleven-year-old from Poland, Maine, wrote to Muskie about the odor of the Little Androscoggin River near her home. She said area residents had written to the governor with no result and urged Muskie to help the situation. A Portland dentist wrote to Senator Muskie, enclosing

Sen. Muskie held almost three dozen public hearings around the country to generate support for the Clean Water Act of 1972. His wife, Jane, is at his left.

photographs of pollution of Casco Bay at the outlet of the Presumpscot River and asking Muskie to act.

The dentist, Richard E. Gosse, wanted industries, especially the paper mill upriver in Westbrook, held accountable for river pollution. Gosse was just one of hundreds of people who wrote to Muskie, expressing their concerns and helping to strengthen his case that the federal government must do something to protect the environment. Muskie's popularity and position as an environmental leader gave him the opportunity to speak about the challenges of dealing with pollution and other problems. In a film clip, Muskie says, "It has been said that pollution is a highly sexy political subject."

He called dealing with pollution a "highly difficult and potentially explosive political opportunity," and noted there were hard choices to be made, especially at the local level. Muskie introduced what came to be known as the Clean Water Act on October 28, 1971. His Senate subcommittee held thirty-three days of hearings over a period of two years in various locations around the country before and after the bill was introduced. The visibility of those hearings brought Muskie even more mail about environmental issues. The legislation that Muskie and the strongly bipartisan committee backed was groundbreaking.

It required zero discharge by 1985. The goal was that nothing of a polluting nature ultimately would be allowed to be dumped into rivers and lakes directly and indirect runoff would be controlled as well. Previously, water pollution was discussed in terms of how much discharge from various sources the body of water could stand. Muskie and the committee believed a goal of no pollution was the best alternative to trying to decide what and how much of various materials would be acceptable in a body of water. He wanted people to be able to go boating, fishing, and swimming.

It gave the Environmental Protection Agency the authority to implement pollution control programs that promoted "biological integrity," a term that became especially important to continued environmental efforts. Adding to the disputes over discharges, cost, and enforcement were political tensions arising from the 1972 Presidential election. Both Ed Muskie, a Democrat, and Richard Nixon, the Republican incumbent, were running for president. Even though Muskie dropped out of the race, accusations of political posturing continued. Nixon was not the only opponent of the bill and the standards it created.

Some environmentalists opposed it as well because they did not trust the experts that the committee had relied on in constructing the bill. They also did not trust the government enforcement agencies such as the Environmental Protection Agency and the Army Corps of Engineers. Many people contributed to writing and marking up the bill, and Muskie worked with colleagues of both political parties to settle on language and provisions before sending the legislation to the floor of the Senate for a vote. It passed 86–0 in the Senate and 380–14 in the House. The House and Senate then spent 39 days in conference to work out their differences. The Conference Committee report was passed with similar large margins. President Richard Nixon vetoed the 1972 Clean Water Act, but on October 18, 1972, the veto was overridden, and the bill became law.

While the no-discharge goal that Muskie and his allies promoted has yet to be achieved, the 1972 Clean Water Act is credited with leading to improved water quality in rivers, lakes and streams. In the years since the bill passed, agricultural and urban runoff have been greatly reduced. While many were concerned about the costs to industry and to employment, the bill did not lead to the dire results some predicted.

9

The Many Facets of Lawmaker Edmund Muskie

This speech was delivered by Leon G. Billings, a long-time Muskie aide and friend, in 2005.[1]

I am delighted to be here this evening to talk about my mentor, my employer and my friend, Edmund S. Muskie. I knew Ed Muskie for nearly thirty-five years. I worked for him for pay for fifteen and for free for fifteen more. I watched him evolve as a politician, as an intellect and as a statesman.

I knew him best and was best known in relation to him with respect to his work on environmental issues. For twelve years of my working tenure, I was his chief environmental aide. I spent three years as his chief of staff in the Senate and at the State Department when he was secretary of state.

My relationship with Senator Muskie was unique in that I was not from Maine and therefore shared none of his political roots. I had little background on what he had done or who he had been before I joined his staff in 1966, seven years after he became a United States senator.

I knew he was a Democrat. I knew he served on the Senate Committee on Public Works. I knew he was interested in pollution. I knew he was considered a moderate. And I knew that he had a relatively low political profile. I had no idea of the power of his intellect, the scope of his interests or the magnitude of his temper.

I watched him grow through his vice -presidential candidacy with Hubert Humphrey in 1968; his failed presidential effort in 1972; and his evolution as a leader in the United States Senate in the last decade of his service. I knew of no one who did not respect Senator Muskie. I knew few who did not fear his temper. And I knew even fewer who had any grasp of the breadth of this giant of his times. One of those few was Don Nicoll, his long-time chief of staff, close friend and, of late, manager of his oral history.

Some knew Ed Muskie more intimately than I because they started out when he began his political career. One knew when someone was an old friend because they called him Ed. I told a story at his funeral about a time not long before his death when we had occasion to have lunch. In casual conversation, I referred to him by his first name. He looked at me and said, “So, it’s Ed now, is it?” For the rest of his life, I only called him “Senator.”

Edmund S. Muskie was indeed a giant of his time. He may have been the most prolific legislator in American history. His legislative record is as diverse as it is prolific. Those few who recall his service will remember him best for his initiation of the worldwide environmental revolution. And it is appropriate that he should be remembered for that because, as I noted in a recent speech for his colleague and friend Howard Baker of Tennessee, he took Congress, the country, and soon the world, to a place it had never been before in a way for which there was no legislative precedent. And I will come back to that.

But did you know that Ed Muskie was one of the principal authors of the War Powers Act which intended to define the relationship between Congress and the Executive with respect to declaration of war? Did you know that Senator Muskie crafted the federal Budget Act which created the Congressional budget process?

Did you know that Senator Muskie wrote the law which has preserved thousands, if not tens of thousands, of historic places in the United States? Did you know that Muskie was the father of modern public housing legislation which replaced the old projects approach to public housing? Did you know that Ed Muskie crafted virtually the entire body of law which dictates the relationships between local, state and federal government? Did you know that he wrote the first "sunset" laws which called for periodic Congressional review of myriad federal laws? I am sure you don't know, and few would remember, that it was Ed Muskie's initiative that opened the federal legislative process so that the public could see how laws were made.

Edmund Muskie did not win the presidency, but he will be remembered as one of the most effective senators of the twentieth century.

Some of you may recall that at one time the United States, as a colonial power, "owned" the Panama Canal. The Carter Administration negotiated a treaty to return the Canal to the Panamanians. In fact, the person who negotiated that treaty was Sol Linowitz, a Cornell Law classmate and lifelong friend of Senator Muskie's.

Because the President knew that there would be widespread opposition to his treaty and doubted the strength of the advocacy of the Senate Foreign Relations Committee, he asked—at the behest, I suspect, of Sol Linowitz—Ed Muskie personally to take on a major role in securing ratification. Muskie argued that his role in the Senate was currently predicated on knowledge of economic policy and suggested that he make the economic argument for approving the Treaty. And Carter agreed.

Eventually, the Treaty was ratified over the deep and strenuous objections of veterans' groups all over the country. Muskie knew that the veterans' groups in Maine were powerful and noisy. So he told President Carter that he would not publicly endorse the Treaty until he had done his homework in the State of Maine. I recall, because I was his chief of staff at the time, that he instructed me to set up a weekend in Maine where he would make a couple of speeches to the public; a speech to Democratic Party activists; and he would meet with the editorial boards of the *Bangor Daily News* and the Portland *Press Herald*. He also scheduled a couple of radio shows.

We came to Maine, and he kept his schedule, including dropping in on out-of-the-way radio stations to just chat on the air. Shortly after we returned to Washington, the *Press Herald* ran a strong editorial in support of the Panama Canal Treaty. Muskie had announced that he would support the Treaty and, even faced with the opposition of the Veterans of Foreign Wars and the American Legion, he stuck to his guns. His then colleague, Senator Bill Cohen, was furious because he felt that Muskie, by going to Maine and gaining public support, had trapped him into supporting the Treaty too. And he did.

This story tells us perhaps as much about Ed Muskie as any I can think of. It tells us that he was a crafty and clever politician. It tells us that he didn't rush into difficult political decisions. It tells us that he knew that he was safer if he solicited and obtained broad support than if he took a position and hoped the electorate would catch up with him. And it tells us that he had the skill to shape an outcome with little political risk. His handling of the Panama Canal Treaty may indeed have been the reason why President Carter was so comfortable in appointing him Secretary of State in 1980.

Muskie will probably always be best remembered because of the "tears in New Hampshire" event, which occurred on the eve of the New Hampshire primary in 1972. What few will remember is that he won the New Hampshire primary and in fact got more than 50 percent of the vote. Today that would be a major victory for any Presidential candidate, but in 1972 the press characterized it as a defeat. What few will forget is that in defense of his wife's reputation and integrity, he became emotional and attacked the *Manchester Union Leader*.

I recall, and would prefer others would remember, his performance in Washington, Pennsylvania, early in his vice -presidential campaign in 1968. Because of the Vietnam War and the boisterous and sometimes violent protests, few politicians would engage the public directly. Before he pulled out of his re-election race, President Johnson campaigned on military bases and in controlled environments, much like George Bush did in the past election. No candidate for President or Vice President had appeared on a major college campus. And few went to any uncontrolled events. Muskie started out his campaign by appearing before a college crowd at the University of San Francisco. It was a smashing success, reported on favorably by the national media—because it had occurred on a college campus.

Shortly thereafter, Muskie made the appearance in Washington, Pennsylvania. It was an open-air event on a stage before a large crowd—who didn't have to have tickets to attend. One very loud and obnoxious young man kept interrupting Muskie's speech, heckling loudly and trying to shout him down. Muskie asked the young man to come up on the stage, which he did. He then said to him, "You clearly have something to say. I will listen to you if you then listen to me."

Both had their say. Muskie received enormous praise for his handling of the situation, and it diffused much of the heckling that would otherwise have occurred during the remainder of his candidacy. Muskie had a rare ability to grasp the moment. And he didn't need staff to tell him when the moment was or how to grasp it. I recall on one occasion, during debate on the Defense Department appropriations bill, someone on the Muskie personal office staff called me and said, "You've got to get over to the floor. The Senator is having a fight with John Stennis on environmental policy."

I rushed to the floor to find he indeed had engaged Stennis, a Mississippi senator who was chairman of the defense committee, on the issue of a Defense Department exemption to the National Environmental Policy Act. Stennis wanted to include an amendment in

The *Captain's Lady* is docked near the juncture of the Merrimack River and the Atlantic Ocean. (*Dan Graovac photo*)

his bill. Senator Muskie's staff had informed him of this amendment by a two-page memo. We had not received any response to the memo, so we had no indication that he intended to debate the issue, nor did we have any opportunity to prepare extensively for a debate should it take place. When I got to the floor, Muskie was engaged in a furious exchange with Senator Stennis. At the end, Stennis withdrew his amendment; Muskie prevailed; and he turned to me, and he said, "Why did you come over?"

I was very proud to be working for Ed Muskie that day, though my ego was a little singed. During and after Muskie's service, many of us told stories of his much-feared temper. His colleagues were reluctant to take him on during debate because they feared he would explode. He once told me after such an event on the Senate floor, "Don't you think I use my temper well?" I had no idea that he was faking, and I'm not sure he did.

My own experiences with his vaunted temper were many. Because I lasted with him almost as long as any other staff person other than the late Gayle Fitzgerald Cory and my friend Don Nicoll, I saw him and his temper from virtually every perspective. I know that at times he used his 6-foot 4-inch frame and the volume of his voice to intimidate. I know that he at times used a demonstration of temper to make a point or try to overwhelm his adversaries. But I also know that often his temper was real and very, very scary.

Another dimension of Ed Muskie of which I wasn't aware for many years was the breadth of his political philosophy. Because I came from Montana, was raised in Montana politics and had had no exposure to Muskie as a legislator or as a Governor and spent very little time with him personally for many of the years I worked for him, I was not aware of the philosophical underpinning which drove his policy direction.

During his ill-fated presidential campaign, we had occasion to hold a hearing on the coast of Delaware at the behest of his friend and colleague, Senator J. Caleb Boggs, a Republican and the ranking member on his Subcommittee. We were accompanied on the plane to the hearing site by Senator Clifford Case of New Jersey, a moderate Republican, and Senator Bill Roth of Delaware, yet another moderate Republican. During that trip, I made an observation about the avaricious role of banking in our society. And I suggested that while it was likely that Senator Muskie held views like Senator Case about banks, I was a prairie populist and came from a background which simply didn't trust banks or bankers. Muskie, in the presence of Case, gave me a lecture about his anti-bank populism as a Maine Democrat, something I wouldn't have known had I not chosen to be provocative.

Another aspect of Muskie which is little known is that he was not pro-choice. The issue of choice, of course, was not significant during much of his political tenure. It came up from time to time in two respects: a Constitutional amendment to ban abortion; and Medicaid funding of abortion. While the Senator questioned the wisdom of amending the Constitution for social purpose, we were never able to convince him that Medicaid funding for abortion was appropriate. He was, after all, a lifelong and devoted Catholic. He did not bring his religion to the office. In fact, I didn't even know he was a practicing Catholic until an occasion on which we were out of town at a field hearing on a Sunday. He disappeared early on Sunday morning, and I found out later that he had gone to Mass. I had been on his staff for four years.

Never once during my fifteen-year tenure with Senator Muskie did the issue of religion come up. I infer from his opposition to Medicaid funding of abortion that it was a function of his religious views, but he never said so. Later in life, long after he left government service, he changed. Not only did he change on the issue of abortion, but he conveniently forgot that he had ever been other than pro-choice. This makes an important point about Ed Muskie. Many believe people's personalities are fully developed when they are very young, and their intellect matures when they are in their twenties. For example, most brilliant physicists and mathematicians are said to peak in their post-graduate years. Ed Muskie's intellect, perception and creativity grew throughout his public life. I watched him change dramatically after he returned from the vice -presidential campaign. While he would disagree, clearly the things he saw, the places he visited, the people he heard made a deep and significant impression on him. And it changed his public policy views.

I once irritated, if not outright angered, him by suggesting that the vice presidential and presidential campaigns had turned him from a small state Senator to a truly national statesman. He, of course, argued vociferously that he'd always been a national politician and that he'd never just been a small-state senator. Again, because I was from "away" and had not seen this man evolve through the state legislature and the governor's office or his early years in the Senate, I could only apply the perspective I had from meeting him in 1963 and joining his staff in 1966. And I can tell you that from my perspective the Ed Muskie who entered the decade of the environment was a very different Ed Muskie than the man I first met in 1963.

When I first went to work for Muskie, he struck me as being cautious to the point of being conservative. I did not understand that he felt the need to carry his colleagues along the journey on which he had been embarked. I was much less wise and had much less appreciation for the need to build a foundation before you build a house. So, it could have been part of a grander plan that caused him to take the giant steps which he initiated following the vice -presidential campaign or perhaps it could have been that he was emboldened by the experience of that campaign. Likely, it was some combination of both.

He came back from the near victory in 1968 to pass a piece of legislation which created the concept of strict, joint and several liability for pollution. Even before Earth Day he and his intellectual peer, Republican Senator Howard Baker of Tennessee, crafted legislation governing cleanup of oil spills, which established a standard in federal law which far exceeded admiralty law, and which guaranteed that the people responsible for oil pollution would pay to clean it up. That bill was as radical as any enacted but the Clean Air Act. When years later Superfund was enacted, the standard for liability was the standard that Muskie and Baker established in April 1970.

He understood the politics of Earth Day and he understood the politics of the national environmental movement and he grasped the opportunity. Later, in 1971, he did for clean water what he had done for clean air. He shifted ground from his earlier objective of establishing water quality standards and building pollution controls to meet these standards to requiring pollution controls and then measuring to see whether quality standards had been achieved.

The 1972 Clean Water Act is known primarily because it established a regulatory program which created a federal discharge reduction program and a similar regulatory program to protect the nation's wetlands. What is not known widely is that the 1972 Clean Water Act also created the circumstances under which the Congressional budget process became essential.

A lone kayaker enjoys the river in Newburyport, near the 1-95 bridge. (*Dan Graovac photo*)

For many years Muskie and his colleagues on the Committee, in both houses and on both sides of the aisle had wanted to increase the level of federal funding for waste treatment plants. Republican governors from the Northeast, like Rockefeller of New York, Sargent of Massachusetts, Agnew of Maryland, all appealed to the Committee to find a source of waste treatment plant funding so they could make critically needed infrastructure improvements. Congress enacted the limited federal grant program in 1966, but the money was distributed largely to small towns in rural areas rather than to the big cities where the real pollution problems existed.

In 1971, Muskie and his colleagues in the Senate made two critically important decisions: first, that the pool of federal funding should be increased to $18 billion; and second, that it should be authorized in a way that made it certain to be appropriated and spent. While there are many other details associated with that legislative initiative, the most important point is that Richard Nixon, knowing that Muskie would not be his opponent in the general election, vetoed the bill and then when, for the first time in his four years in office, the veto was overridden, impounded $9 billion of the construction grant money.

This impoundment led to litigation by the City of New York and others. A little-known historical fact is that much of the brief before the Supreme Court that was filed by the City of New York was crafted by Muskie Subcommittee counsel, now a member of the Maine Law Court, Don Alexander. The Supreme Court held that the President did not have legal authority to impound appropriations made by the Congress. This was dramatic and enormously significant because for generations presidents had simply refused to spend money Congress appropriated. The fact that the president could no longer just refuse to spend money Congress appropriated meant for the first time Congress would have to better discipline itself in its spending habits.

Historically, Congress voted all manner of expenditures knowing that their carefree ways would be disciplined by an executive branch which had to keep an eye on issues like the capacity to spend appropriated funds and the federal deficit.

Faced with the Supreme Court's decision that the executive branch did not have authority to not spend Congressionally appropriated funds, Muskie crafted the Budget Act. The budget law was intended to establish the parameters which would govern the appropriation of funds by the Congress. In theory, the Budget Act would say how much could be spent and how much the deficit would be and what, if any, new revenue had to be generated to balance the books. Because there was no constitutional requirement that the budget be balanced, the latter was more an exercise in controlling the size of the deficit.

Like pollution policy, Muskie mastered budget policy. His diligence, his attention to detail and his sense of Senatorial responsibility made him a perfect choice to develop and implement the initial budget process. For a liberal Democrat he had—perhaps unique among liberals—a rare capacity to sit through endless hours of hearings on economic detail. As he had, for so many years as chairman of the Environment Subcommittee, listened to endless hours of technical detail on science and technology of pollution, he now listened to economists and accountants and the policy people who wanted to spend federal money.

He would go home at night lugging two and sometimes three 3-inch binders containing memos on every subject area of the federal budget. It was his habit to get up early in the morning, often around 5 a.m., and read this material until he left for the office around 9 a.m. He was better prepared than his colleagues and he insisted on knowing more than the witnesses that would appear before him.

It was often said of his presidential running mate and close friend, Hubert Humphrey, that Humphrey had more answers than there were questions. Muskie always had more questions than there were answers, and it well behooved his staff to be able to respond.

The budget process wasn't just an exercise in balancing the books. It required a political skill, and it engaged his social conscience. With respect to political skill he had, as his ranking committee member, a conservative Republican from Oklahoma named Henry Bellmon. Bellmon may have been the most conservative of the allies Muskie engaged over his tenure. He was at least as conservative as Senator Jim Buckley of New York, who served as ranking member on the Environment Subcommittee for several years. Muskie knew that to keep Bellmon on his side on issues like defense spending he needed to compromise on social spending. He chose to take a stand on the school lunch program. Then Senator George McGovern had a budget amendment which would have added funding to the budget for school lunches.

Morning fog meets with warming sunshine on the Merrimack. (*Dan Graovac photo*)

To the surprise and dismay of his liberal colleagues, Muskie opposed McGovern. But he gained the cooperation of Senator Bellmon in opposing excessive increases in defense spending. So successful was this gambit that Senator John Stennis, the Mississippi senator who controlled defense spending, solicited and received a private meeting with Muskie. He asked for and received a commitment to a 3 percent increase in defense spending—far below what Muskie had any reason to expect him to request. But Muskie would not waiver on his commitment to social security. In 1979 his Budget Committee staff, both policy and economic, urged him to place limits on the growth of social security payments. He argued, with force, that too many seniors relied on social security as their primary source of income; that he would not be the sponsor of limits on their payments.

Let me conclude with yet another perspective on Senator Muskie. The people of Maine knew him as a national leader, as a creative legislator and as a partisan Democrat. He was one of a very small group of people who built the modern Democratic Party in Maine. He was intensely partisan in his effort to elect Democrats from local government to the White House. In the 1970s there was a state Democratic convention at which Muskie was honored. He was presented with a telephone booth to memorialize his oft-repeated comment that when he began in Maine politics the eastern Democratic Party could fit into a phone booth. I don't know how many times I heard that comment. The legislator Muskie was very different. It was almost as if partisanship stopped at the Maine border. Muskie not only worked with his Republican colleagues, but he sought out special relationships in order to accomplish his legislative objectives.

While he would do everything in his power to defeat a Republican running for office from Maine, he had a remarkably good relationship with Senator Bill Cohen.

But more important was the extent to which he would go to build bipartisan support for his legislative endeavors, whether it was government operations, where he built a working and productive relationship with Senator Bill Roth of Delaware; or the Budget Committee, where he had a special working relationship with the conservative Henry Bellmon from Oklahoma; or the Environment Subcommittee, where variably he had constructive and productive relationships with Republican Senators like moderates J. Caleb Boggs of Delaware and Howard Baker of Tennessee or conservatives like Jim Buckley of New York.

Muskie had a unique skill at developing a relationship with these political adversaries which led to frequent and consistent unanimous support for his legislative initiatives. In so doing, he did not compromise principle. He personified the concept that legislation is the art of the possible. He insisted that the man who was in the middle was in control and was an absolute master of defining the extremes so he could place himself in the middle. In so doing, he brought his colleagues in support of progressive and innovative legislation, much of which passed the Senate without dissent.

10

Two New England Senators Brought You Clean Water-Muskie and Mitchell

This was a newspaper column written for *The Daily News* in Newburyport by author Dyke Hendrickson in 2020.

Those who enjoy the lakes, rivers, bays, and the ocean have two august New England senators to thank for clean water that makes healthy recreation possible: Sen. Edmund S. Muskie and Sen. George J. Mitchell, both of Maine.

The year 2020 marks the fiftieth year of the modern environmental law-making, defined here as the creation of the federal Environmental Protection Agency (Dec. 2, 1970). Through the EPA and the political process, Muskie and Mitchell were two effective leaders in the fight to fund programs designed to produce clean water.

Muskie, who served in the Senate from 1959 to 1980, led the drive to pass the Clean Water Act of 1972. Mitchell, who served 1980 to 1996, was the architect of the Clean Water Amendments in 1987. This was a compromise package that saved clean-water funding when President Ronald Reagan proposed to end federal grants for sewage-treatment plants.

In appreciating these legislative achievements, it should be noted that the "environmental movement" is relatively young. It wasn't recognized until the early '60s, when Rachel Carson's *Silent Spring* brought attention to the dangers of noxious chemicals and their damaging effects on wildlife and natural habitat.

And in a shocking development in 1969, the Cuyahoga River near Cleveland caught fire. The attendant publicity caused a public outcry, and Muskie emerged as the leading voice for clean water in the 1970s. Muskie (1914–1996) was a native of Rumford and had grown up near the polluted Androscoggin River. As a senator, Muskie was known for thoroughly studying issues and basing his arguments for legislation on the facts he gathered.

Muskie shepherded the 1963 Clean Air Act through Congress and stood close to President Lyndon Johnson as he signed the landmark law. When the polluted Cuyahoga River caught fire, Muskie's crusade for clean water drew a larger audience. Muskie's reputation as a steward of the environment earned him the nickname "Mr. Clean" and drew letters from people around the country seeking his support for clean air and clean water causes.

Muskie introduced what came to be known as the Clean Water Act in October 1971. His Senate subcommittee held thirty-three days of hearings over a period of two years in locations around the country. Muskie worked with colleagues of both parties to settle on language and provisions before sending the legislation to the floor of the Senate for a vote. It passed 86-0 in the Senate and 380-14 in the House. President Richard Nixon vetoed the 1972 Clean Water Act, but on October 18, 1972, the veto was overridden, and the bill became law. The 1972 Clean Water Act, by offering millions in federal grants to municipal authorities for sewage-treatment plants, is credited with providing improved water quality in rivers, lakes and the ocean.

Mitchell was also a major leader in the funding of clean-water projects. In the late '80s, President Reagan wanted to cease giving grants that financed treatment plants and other clean-water initiatives. Mitchell, who had grown up in Waterville on the polluted Kennebec River, led the drive to maintain funding for clean water. He was able to keep the program alive, albeit in a weaker version. The amendments to the Clean Water Act of 1972 were passed in 1987. It is sometimes down as the Water Quality Act of 1987.

The amendments provided low-interest loans—not grants—to communities that sought financial support. It is now known as the Clean Water State Revolving Fund. Interest rate in 2019 was 1.5 percent, according to federal figures. Mitchell retired from the Senate in 1996. But he returned in 2002 to speak to a Senate committee on public

Former Sen. George Mitchell, like Muskie a Democrat from Maine, was instrumental in creating low-interest loans that would enable communities to clean their rivers.

health. The transcript of his remarks is excerpted here because it encompasses the thoughts of both Mitchell and Muskie.

Mitchell said:

> As I prepared my testimony for this hearing, I was struck by the similarity in the debate over clean water in 1972, 1987 and today. In 1972 and in 1987, the bills survived Presidential vetoes. In each case, cost was a significant issue. In each case, the nation's desire for clean water overshadowed all other issues. I believe that is still the case. The words that Senator Muskie used in 1972 in urging passage of the original Clean Water Act apply to today's challenges, and I would like to quote them for you briefly.

Mitchell quoted Muskie as saying the following:

> Can we afford clean water? Can we afford rivers and lakes and oceans which continue to make life possible on the planet? Can we afford life itself? The answers are the same. Those questions were never asked as we destroyed the waters of our nation, and they deserve no answers as we finally move to restore and renew them. The questions answer themselves. We have reached a point in our struggle against water pollution where, as we say in New England, "We must either fish or cut bait." If we are serious about restoring the quality of our nation's waters to a level that will support life in the future, then we ought to be prepared to make some sacrifices in that effort now.

In 2023, those who enjoy the outdoors can credit two of New England's most committed, effective senators for a cleaner and safer environment.

11

American Rivers Assesses the Merrimack

American Rivers, a non-profit organization based in Washington, D.C., gains national headlines every year for identifying some of the most polluted rivers in the country. It brings attention to the shortcomings of officials who are supposed to keep the rivers clean. It also makes recommendations on how a river can improve. In 2016, American Rivers named the Merrimack River to the Most Endangered List. Here were some of the organization's comments that year:

Birthplace of American industry, drinking water source for over a half million people, and home to Eastern brook trout and other fish and wildlife, the Merrimack River is one of New England's treasures. However, its forests are disappearing, cut down to make way for developments, roads and parking lots.

Unless the EPA acts now to protect sensitive lands and implement green infrastructure solutions, the river and its communities will be choked by increasingly polluted runoff.

The health of the 117-mile Merrimack River and its 11 major tributaries is of great importance to 2 million residents and an abundance of fish and wildlife species.

Currently, thousands depend on the river for drinking water, including consumers in Lowell, Lawrence, Tewksbury, Methuen, and Andover, in Massachusetts and Nashua, N.H. Two more cities in New Hampshire, Manchester and Concord, plan to do so soon.

In addition, the Merrimack is historically important as one of the birthplaces for industrialization, with the river powering textile mills and other factories. The region "was then to industry what the Silicon Valley is today," said Theodore Steinburg, author of "Nature Incorporated: Industrialization and the Waters of New England." Today, 847 dams harness the river and its tributaries, and some are candidates for removal to help restore river health and fisheries.

The Merrimack River is one of the three most important large rivers on the East Coast in its conservation value to migratory river herring and one of the six most important for twelve migratory fish species. The Merrimack watershed also supports at least seventy-five state and federally listed endangered species, numerous pairs of bald eagles, the largest tidal marsh habitat in New England, and a portion of the Atlantic Flyway bird migration route.

Eagles have been returning to the Merrimack, where they can fish in open water.

The Threat

Pavement is rapidly replacing trees across the Merrimack River watershed. The impact of unsustainable development on land, forests, habitat, and water quality is the largest threat that the Merrimack River watershed faces today.

The U.S. Forest Service ranks the Merrimack River watershed as the most threatened in the country due to the development of forest lands, fourth for associated threats to water quality, and seventh for loss of habitat for species at risk. An estimated 40 to 63 percent of the private forested land in the watershed is projected to be developed by 2030.

These threats are the direct result of the growing population and associated development occurring throughout the watershed, especially in southern New Hampshire, the most rapidly developing part of the state. For example, the average population growth rate between 2000 and 2010 in the three main New Hampshire counties of the Merrimack River watershed (Belknap, Merrimack, and Hillsborough) is nearly two times greater than the New England average.

Protecting the extensive forests in the Merrimack River watershed is essential to preserve their natural filtration function, which removes nutrients, pathogens, and other pollutants in order to help clean the river's water. The looming loss of these forests threatens the water supply of the more than 600,000 people who depend directly on

At left is Gen. Ben Butler's Toothpick, a low-tech navigation guide on the river. Butler was a Civil War general, governor of Massachusetts, and a resident of Lowell.

the Merrimack River for their drinking water today, along with the additional 200,000 residents expected to use the water soon.

Pollutants that flow though the Merrimack watershed ultimately impact the Gulf of Maine's marine ecosystem. In fact, the Merrimack is already the second greatest contributor of nitrogen and phosphorus to the Gulf of Maine. In the coming years, the National Oceanic and Atmospheric Administration predicts an increase in rainfall and flooding for New England rivers due to climate change, which will only increase polluted runoff. With the continued transformation of these vitally important forested lands into suburban developments, the ability of the land to absorb, hold, and naturally clean stormwater will be greatly reduced. The loss of forested lands also reduces habitat for threatened and endangered species.

What Must Be Done

In order to ensure clean drinking water and protect fish and wildlife in the Merrimack River from poorly planned development, the U.S. Environmental Protection Agency (EPA) needs to create a regional watershed team and implement key safeguards including protection for important forest lands along rivers and streams, green infrastructure solutions, and improved stormwater management to reduce the excess nutrients and pathogens in the river.

The EPA has created watershed teams in other basins facing chronic water quality challenges including the Chesapeake Bay, Great Lakes, and Gulf of Mexico. Such an approach empowers local citizens to take greater responsibility for river stewardship.

An aerial view of the Haverhill–Amesbury area. Demographers say rapid residential growth causes the removal of fields and forests, components of a strong river system.

Currently, EPA is already working closely with the City of Lawrence, Merrimack River Watershed Council, the Commonwealth of Massachusetts, and other partners to improve Lawrence's water. Now is the time to take the action to the next level. Local officials have a once-in-a-lifetime opportunity to make a lasting positive impact on the Merrimack by facilitating and funding a plan, backed by local citizens, to conserve the river through smart planning and accelerated land protection while there is still time.

12

Those Cleaning the Merrimack Can Look to Success in North Carolina

In late 2022, American Rivers, the non-profit environmental organization in Washington, D.C., named the Neuse River of North Carolina the "River of the Year" in the U.S. The 275-mile waterway was recognized for reducing pollution and for bringing disparate organizations together to work for a healthier river. American Rivers in 2007 had named it one of the ten "most vulnerable" waterways in the country. The honor in 2022 noted its significant improvement. Perhaps those attempting to clean the Merrimack today can learn from the "best practices" of those in North Carolina.[1]

I recently traveled to North Carolina to see the river and meet the people who are improving it. Here are several useful developments at the Neuse that officials in the Merrimack River corridor might consider in their effort to clean our river.

Riverkeepers. The Neuse employs a riverkeeper of the upper Neuse and one for the lower Neuse. They are unofficial ombudsmen who respond to concerns that residents and workers report. If there has been a chemical spill, a riverkeeper can contact the Department of Environmental Protection, and work with state and federal officials to clean it. Riverkeepers also report the incident on their webpage and print newsletters, so residents will be aware. If a spring clean-up of riverbanks is scheduled or a fund-raising program is launched, the riverkeepers can spread the word to its database of several thousand. The Neuse's two riverkeepers are employed by Sound Rivers, a non-profit that receives funds from federal, state and local sources. It also receives grants from private institutions.

Zoning assistance. A major need for many river communities is help in overseeing construction near the river. Sound Rivers has created zoning ordinances that communities can emulate so there are laws in place when developers consider projects. Construction that reduces trees and fields is one of the threats to the health of modern rivers.

Teaming with schools. Sound Rivers has launched programs that help schools "adopt" part of the river. Youngsters can pick up trash, or plant trees and bushes along the banks to cut down on erosion.

Linking with the private sector. Many businesses and corporations rely on a clean river with drinkable water. By enlisting private companies in the clean-up efforts, work

The 275-mile Neuse River in North Carolina was named "River of the Year" by an environmental group in 2022.

projects are completed, and financial grants are realized. About 2.5 million people get their drinking water from the Neuse.

In 2016, the 117-mile-long Merrimack River was named as one of the ten most vulnerable rivers. American Rivers said that the river is threatened by combined sewer overflows (CSOs), a growing number of construction projects (especially in New Hampshire) and the presence of "forever" chemicals that enter the river from business and industry. Perhaps the Massachusetts and New Hampshire organizations that have an interest in the Merrimack can organize efforts in the continuing attempt to clean the river. More than 600,000 residents on the North Shore get their drinking water from the Merrimack and untold thousands use it for fishing, boating and (sometimes) swimming. The Merrimack might even strive to be "river of the year," which could be an added incentive for those committed to this historic waterway.

13

Why the Neuse Was Named River of the Year

On the fiftieth anniversary of the Clean Water Act, a North Carolina river is making a comeback. This article was part of a statement from American Rivers.

American Rivers is excited to announce the Neuse River as our 2022 River of the Year. The Neuse has seen major progress in recent decades, with cleanup efforts improving water quality and restoration efforts improving habitat for wildlife and access for fishing and boating. The river's rebounding health has benefited wildlife and people alike, and as the nation celebrates the 50th anniversary of the Clean Water Act this year, the Neuse illustrates how positive steps for clean water benefit both the environment and economy.

Returning a river to good health does not happen overnight, nor is it a guarantee moving forward. For us to continue celebrating the Neuse as a regional and national treasure, we must remain diligent and pay attention to threats to the river. The growing effects of climate change are continually putting new stresses on the river and its water supplies, and we must ensure that the benefits of a healthier river are enjoyed equitably among the communities in the watershed, especially communities of color that have faced systemic environmental injustice and continue to bear the brunt of river pollution and increased flooding.

About the Neuse

The iconic Neuse River's name is derived from the Neusiok people, who once lived near the mouth of the river, and means "peace river," likely because of its slow-moving nature in contrast to the powerful Cape Fear to the south. The Neuse watershed is also the traditional territory of numerous other tribes including the Lumbee, the Skaruhreh/Tuscarora, the Saponi, the Occaneechi, and the Cheraw.

Flowing 275 miles from the Piedmont of North Carolina to Pamlico Sound on the Atlantic coast, the headwaters are located at the confluence of the Eno and Little Rivers, just before flowing through Falls Lake Reservoir outside of Durham, N.C. The

Those working for a cleaner river own a vessel used by riverkeepers there.

main stem pours out of the 12,000-acre Falls Lake Reservoir—a well-loved recreation destination and the drinking water source for half a million people—at Raleigh, NC. In the upper part of the watershed, the river runs fast, with rocky whitewater, riffles and shallow pools, but on its path to the sea, the Neuse widens and slows. Numerous smaller streams flow into the Neuse, including Crabtree Creek, Walnut Creek, Swift Creek, Little River, Contentnea Creek, and the Trent River, connecting the Neuse with communities across its more than 6,200-square-mile watershed.

The river provides drinking water for the vast majority of the approximately 2.5 million people—a quarter of North Carolina's population—who currently reside in the 77 established communities within its watershed. Of the 3.5 million acres that comprise the Neuse basin, 48,000 acres are state parks, 110,000 acres are game lands held by the Wildlife Resources Commission, and 58,000 acres are National Forest.

The Neuse River Greenway Trail winds along the river as part of NC's Mountains-to-Sea Trail that runs from the Great Smoky Mountains to the Outer Banks. The Neuse River Blueway goes past the impressive 100-foot Cliffs of the Neuse canyon. The Neuse flows through a remote portion of cypress swamp and hardwood forest the locals call the "LetLones." It was thought to be so full of moonshine stills and poisonous snakes it got the reputation for being best left alone.

Recreation on the Neuse

The Neuse meets the Pamlico Sound just beyond New Bern, the original capital of the state, founded in 1710 and a center of maritime and agricultural commerce at the time. There, the river becomes brackish with wind-driven tides, and widens to become the widest river in the country—about 6 miles across at the town of Oriental. At its

The Neuse River offers fast-moving water for canoers.

confluence with the Pamlico Sound, the Neuse River joins one of the most productive estuaries in the country and the largest lagoonal estuary in the world.

As quarter of North Carolina's population live in the Neuse basin, and the river provides drinking water for most of them. These locals have been connected to the river for centuries, building a culture of fishing and boating from tubes and kayaks in the headwaters, to large sailboats and fishing boats in the estuary. Today, the watershed is home to both North Carolina's historic agricultural and manufacturing economies and its new, robust information technology and pharmaceutical economy. The density of people, along with the diversity of industries between growing urbanized centers and critical agricultural lands, make it critically important to resolve water resource issues facing the watershed.

Water Quality Improvements

The federal Clean Water Act, signed into law in 1972, has driven most of the improvements for the Neuse River and the communities that rely on it. The Act stemmed the dumping of untreated pollution into the river and the state and communities along it rallied to the Act's ambitious call to make the river "fishable and swimmable" for everyone. This meant textile mills and other manufacturing had to clean up their discharges, putting a stop to the kind of pollution in the Neuse and its tributaries that famously caused it to run different colors depending on what was being dyed that day.

In the area where the Neuse nears the Atlantic, a drawbridge operates to permit larger craft to reach the ocean. (*Dyke Hendrickson photo*)

Recent cleanup efforts on the Neuse were catalyzed by a series of fish kills in the mid-1990s that were attributed to excessive pollution coming from sewage treatment facilities and untreated urban and agricultural stormwater run-off. This pollution created toxic algal outbreaks along the river and in the estuary that killed millions of fish. The ensuing cleanup plans improved water quality by reducing pollution from the sewage treatment plants, including significant investments by the large cities along the Neuse, like Raleigh, which built and now operates a state-of-the-art facility.

The communities in the upper Neuse River watershed are forging a new course for improving clean water supplies and meeting the goals of the Clean Water Act. In 2015, the communities began developing the new approach based on sound science and delivering benefits to human and natural communities. The new regulatory structure reimagines the regulatory structure to stress investing in practices that restore natural function to rivers and streams and provide numerous benefits to improving clean water. The watershed has also seen the value in protecting critical watershed lands for the preservation of water quality over the last twenty years. The upper portion of the watershed is one of the fastest growing in the nation with huge development pressures for new housing.

The state of North Carolina has invested more than $68 million through the NC Land and Water Fund (once the Clean Water Management Trust Fund) in protecting land in the watershed, and an additional $75 million restoring the river and improving clean water. A recent example: the state's buyout of over one thousand acres of remote wilderness along the Neuse River lowlands in the Brogden Bottomlands—one of the last vestiges of wilderness in the rapidly growing Triangle. This has been supplemented by the City of Raleigh's innovative source water protection plan that allocates $0.15 per 1,000 gallons of water used and has invested more than $10 million to protect prioritized watershed properties. This idea has spread in recent years to other communities, with Durham also initiating investments in watershed protection in the last five years.

Coal Ash Pond Cleanup

Duke Energy constructed the HF Lee Power Station in 1951, on the banks of the Neuse River just upstream of the city of Goldsboro. The plant, which had three coal-fired units, was retired in 2012. Over its functional life the power plant dumped more than 6 million tons of coal ash into unlined pits along the Neuse riverbank. The horrific spill of coal ash into the Dan River in 2014 resulted in a renewed effort to eliminate these threats statewide, which led to closing the storage pit on the Neuse.

In 2020, an agreement was reached between Sound Rivers, the Southern Environmental Law Center and other state non-profits, along with Duke Energy and the NC Department of Environmental Quality to excavate and recycle all of the coal ash stored along the Neuse by 2035. As of April 2022, Duke Energy has removed over 400,000 tons of coal from the banks of the Neuse River.

Dam Removal

For years, antiquated dams blocked the Neuse River, harming water quality and habitat for fish and wildlife. But today the Neuse is a river reborn, thanks to the 1998 removal of the Quaker Neck Dam outside of Goldsboro and the 2017 removal of Milburnie Dam in Raleigh. These removals were triggered through the regulatory process under the federal Clean Water Act as they offset unstoppable impacts in other parts of the watershed. The removal of the dams improved water quality, creating cooler, more natural river flows. Now the river flows freely from Falls Lake Reservoir all the way to the Atlantic, making it one of the longest free-flowing rivers in the Southeast.

Neuse River Needs to Improve

As impressive as it is, the story of the Neuse River's restoration is not complete. While the Clean Water Act has delivered major benefits, it still hasn't fully delivered on its promise of fishable and swimmable waters. The added pressures from the rapid pace of development, an increase in densely packed industrial hog and poultry operations, and climate change threaten to undercut the progress that has been made. The river and its communities experience spikes of bacterial pollution after most significant rains, as discharge from outdated septic and faulty sewage systems backflow in urban and low-lying areas and flooded industrial hog waste lagoons and spray field runoff contaminate waterways in rural communities. Addressing the environmental injustice of industrial agricultural practices needs to happen to fulfill the promise of the Clean Water

Act. The Neuse River watershed has one of the largest concentrations of Concentrated Animal Feeding Operations (CAFOs) in the country, rivaled only by its neighbor watershed to the south, the Cape Fear. The operations of those CAFOs have created a significant environmental injustice legacy due to the mismanagement of the waste ponds and spray fields that cause bacterial infections, polluted streams, and community disinvestment due to odor contamination. The neighbors of many of these facilities are often people of color who only see the negative impacts of CAFOs and receive no benefits from their operation. The Clean Water Act can provide the tools to reform these practices and balance the benefits across the community.

As a result of ongoing under-regulated development, the Neuse also suffers from dirty water laden with sediment run off due to disturbances to the land around it. Too often large swaths of critical land right along the streams that feed the Neuse are being clearcut, graded and paved, and too many exceptions to environmentally protective rules are made, regularly causing them to lose their effectiveness. The conversion of green spaces to impervious surfaces from development increases the events of community flooding, not just from major storms like hurricanes, but also from the more intense seasonal storms, where more rain is dropped than can be absorbed by the land.

14

Paul Aziz, Skipper on the Yankee Clipper

This newspaper story by Dyke Hendrickson appeared in *The Daily News* of Newburyport in the summer of 2022. It is an interview with a nautical professional who, in summer, spends almost every day on the Merrimack.

Extended hot weather might not be good for lawns and gardens, but it appears to be working for Yankee Clipper Harbor Tours on the Newburyport waterfront. Business has been good this summer. In fact, owner-captain Paul Aziz is planning to launch a second boat in several weeks that will alternate between trips in Haverhill and excursions to the Parker River National Wildlife Refuge.

"Last summer was rainy, and we got off to a slow start," said Aziz, who has owned the business since 2006.

"This year has been good, with people in town and a real interest in getting out on the water. I don't captain every trip, though. Right now, I am getting another boat ready for Coast Guard inspection."

The Yankee Clipper is about 45 feet long and carries about forty-five passengers. It is powered by two 250-horsepower outboard engines. Most trips last about an hour, but there is a ninety-minute sunset cruise, and a three-hour circumnavigation of Plum Island. Also offered is a tour of the Parker River National Wildlife Refuge, which is run at high tide.

"The tour of the Wildlife Refuge generally fills up the boat," said Aziz, who is a high-school science teacher in Topsfield during the school year. "People's interest in the natural world has really increased in recent years. The new boat will be called the Rachel Carson to mark the memory of the early environmentalist."

Carson wrote the book, *Silent Spring*, which is considered one of the first warnings of environmental damage taking place without some government oversight. That was published in 1962. However, in 1947 Carson spent the autumn studying black ducks at the Parker River National Wildlife Refuge. The number of ducks was diminishing, in part because of pressure from duck hunters. Carson, who was a staff researcher for the federal Fish and Wildlife Service at the time, is credited with helping develop a compromise that would accommodate both birth hunters and bird watchers.

The Yankee Clipper, run by Captain Paul Aziz, introduces the river to thousands of tourists each summer. Pictured is Kylene Aziz, niece of the skipper. (*Courtesy photo*)

History is stressed on the tours of the river. The first European to traverse the river was Samuel de Champlain of France in 1605, but the English settled the area. Newbury was founded in 1635, and a new town, called Newburyport, was created by "water-siders" in 1764. Newburyport is the birthplace of the Coast Guard (1790), and the Merrimack River was one of the most prosperous shipbuilding and trading ports in the young republic.

Historians say the "golden age" of Newburyport lasted from about 1790 to 1810. It ended when the "great fire" of 1811 destroyed much of the downtown, and the War of 1812 brought the loss of local ships and cargoes. Many of the stately mansions on High Street and other avenues were built in this period.

Mills that powered the Industrial Revolution began appearing on the river in the 1820s. In part because of the mills' dumping of waste into the river, the Merrimack was a polluted waterway in the nineteenth and part of the twentieth centuries. After the passage of the Clean Water Act in 1972, the river began getting cleaner. Though CSOs (combined sewer overflows) occasionally foul the waterway these days, many visitors enjoy an outing on the Merrimack.

A memorial on the boardwalk in Newburyport contains the names of young mariners lost at sea since 2000.

"I liked hearing about the history of Newburyport," said Sandy Farland, of Hudson, N.H., who was a passenger on the Aziz vessel recently. "And you get a good view of the city from the boat."

Trudy Dooner, of Groveland, also a passenger this week, said, "I enjoyed being on the water on a warm sunny day. We had family from New Jersey here, and we all learned a lot of history."

The Yankee Clipper often heads east from its boardwalk location and enters the Atlantic for a brief time. The history of Plum Island is reviewed. Good things began happening on Plum Island in the early twentieth century. Yankee Clipper pilot Fred Latta noted that the Parker River National Wildlife Refuge, a part of Plum Island, got a start in 1928 when a birdwatcher from Stoneham named Annie Brown gave close to $100,000 so that acreage could be bought and preserved. The federal government created the Wildlife Refuge in 1942. Aziz says that the hour-long trip on the Merrimack enables him and other captains to talk about natural developments of Plum Island and the river.

"I like to stress the value of the estuary and the marsh when considering the health of the ocean," said Aziz, who sometimes hosts student charters. "Much of what we pass in the boat is part of the life cycle, and it is important for the whole area. Also, I talk about the erosion near the water, and the challenges of living at a low sea-level."

15

Merri-Mar Mariners Created a Life on Merrimack

This newspaper story by Dyke Hendrickson appeared in *The Daily News* of Newburyport in the fall of 2022.

It is said that the best two moments of a boater's life are when the vessel is purchased and when it is sold. But there is another poignant moment for owners, especially in a region with a short boating season: The time when the craft is pulled out of the water for the year. The arrival of September marks the beginning of the end of the summer boating season. The first vessels start coming out in mid-month. This has been happening at the Merri-Mar Yacht Basin on Merrimac Street for sixty-six years now. It is one of the oldest family-owned boatyards in the region, and owner Jay Lesynski II is ready for the cycle to begin again.

"We've had an awesome season," said Lesynski, who took over the business from his father and mother. "If there is a positive thing about COVID, it is that it has brought out a lot of people. This is a busy time for boating on the Merrimack. We don't have any vacancies." The yard offers seventy slips.

The story goes that Jay's father, Wally Lesysnki, and his mother, Ruthann, in 1966 took over a property on Merrimac Street known as the Hathaway Boatyard. It had once been the site of the Carrier-Townsend Shipyard, a legendary nineteenth-century builder that manufactured the *Dreadnaught*. The *Dreadnaught* is said to have been the fastest tall ship to cross the Atlantic in the mid-nineteenth century. In 1853, it sailed from New York to Cobb Island, Ireland, in a record-setting nine days, seventeen hours, according to a plaque on the property at the corner of Merrimac and Ashland streets.

When Jay graduated from Newburyport High School in 1979, he began working in his father's business. His son, Jay III, has entered the family business as well. Newburyport Harbor hosts has numerous boatyards and/or yacht clubs, including the American Yacht Club, Bridge Marina, Cove Marina, Hilton's Marina, Newburyport Boat Basin, Newburyport Harbor Marina, North End Boat Club, Ring's Island Marina, and the Windward Yacht Club.

Each facility provides its own range of services, and the Merri-Mar facility seems to offer just about everything. The enterprise is a broker of used boats. It sells merchandise, and it repairs engines. It stores boats in winter.

Sunset on the lower Merrimack, where moored vessels spend the night. (*Dan Graovac photo*)

Several years ago, it underwrote a major expansion of the sales and services facility. "We needed to expand," said Lesynski. The year 2022 represents a high-water mark in pleasure boating on the Merrimack.

"The river is full," said harbormaster Paul Hogg recently. "The private marinas don't have any empty slips, and the moorings on the river itself are all taken. This has been a very busy summer."

About 1,500 vessels are registered with the harbormaster in Newburyport. Hundreds more are in Amesbury and Salisbury, while scores of vessels are launched at Cashman Park each week after being brought in on trailers. Fred Salas, a boat owner from Guilford, N.H., who keeps his 48-foot Hatteras moored at Merri-Mar, said, "This is a good boatyard. The spot itself is protected, and it's like a community with owners and staff helping each other. It's a good place to hang out. If I were in the Caribbean, my dinghy would be stolen. Certainly, the engine would be gone."

One reason for the growth in boating is that the water is cleaner than it was decades ago. Starting with the Clean Water Act of 1972, the Merrimack carries less effluent than it did in the days when mills and factories dumped waste directly into the river.

"We walked down to the end of our pier recently," said Lesynski II. "You could see clearly down to the bottom, about 10 or 15 feet. When I was growing up, a lot of parents didn't want their kids going near the river. They said it was too polluted. A clean river has brought many people to this community, and boaters go to restaurants, go shopping and spend money here."

Lesynski said one of the today's challenges is finding workers. He finds it difficult to hire willing hands. The veteran mariner also expressed concern that small boatyards are being purchased by institutional investors or large boating chains. Lesynski has

The view from Moseley Woods Park, Newburyport, offers scenic views to the west.

developed a flourishing business on the Merrimack but added that more public attention should be paid to the river.

"Dredging the river (to ensure smooth navigation) has been an issue for years," said Lesynksi, who has his own sailboat in one of the slips. "The funding for a dredging project is being discussed now but public officials should have an ongoing plan" for the river's health and navigation.

Still, it appears these are the good old days for this venerable business owner who has spent his whole life on the Merrimack. "What I've enjoyed most over the years is helping our boaters have a good time," he said. "Boat owners are a special group—they love it, whether it's being on the water or puttering around the boat when it's on land. It's been a great business for me, and now I am glad my son has followed me into the family business."

16

Some of the Women Who Worked for a Cleaner River

This story by Dyke Hendrickson appeared in *The Daily News* of Newburyport in the summer of 2022.

Two elected officials who greatly helped the Merrimack River will have left their posts by the end of this year.

State Sen. Diana DiZoglio (D-Methuen), did not run for re-election. Newburyport Mayor Donna Holaday also left public office after being a major advocate for more than a decade. A third supporter, also a woman, left the river (and the earth), more than a century ago. Her name was Ellen Swallow Richards (1842–1911), and she led a team to improve drinking water at the end of the nineteenth century.

The contributions of these three women come to mind as another season of boating, fishing and swimming (upriver) nears an end. Periodic pollution in the river is a continuing problem, as is the inability of the body politic to sustain a serious effort to clean the 117-mile waterway. Most people love the river. Recreational opportunities are many. And if you dwell within view of the Merrimack, it is an awesome sight. For those who walk or drive, numerous scenic sites are available in scores of communities in Massachusetts and New Hampshire.

But cleaning it has proved to be a difficult undertaking. The Clean Water Act of 1972 was a major impetus, because it offered federal grants so riverside communities could build sewage-treatment plants. Those grants disappeared with President Ronald Reagan in 1987. Now there are low-interest loans to help update plants, but numerous communities have been slow to obtain the money.

To paraphrase (and fracture) a remark made by Winston Churchill decades ago about Russia, successful cleansing of the Merrimack appears to be "a riddle wrapped in a mystery inside an enigma." Or, why is it so hard to create an "all-hands-on-deck initiative" to clean the historic waterway?

Heavy rains in recent weeks have resulted in enormous releases of combined sewer overflows (CSOs) into the river. Everyone knows this, but an urgency to improve the situation appears absent among current lawmakers.

Above left: Ellen Swallow Richards, a hydrologist in the late nineteenth century, saved many lives in Lawrence by working with a team to create safe drinking water.

Above right: Annie Brown, a bird-lover from Stoneham, left enough money in her will in the late 1920s for birding clubs to buy much of the southern part of Plum Island. The land she saved is now part of the Parker River National Wildlife Refuge.

DiZoglio was a force in bringing disparate groups together for action. She led an initiative to create the Merrimack River District Commission. One result is that communities must report when they have had CSOs at their plants—and how much effluent was released. DiZoglio also urged treatment plant operators and Environmental Protection Agency officials to be more transparent about their work. At regional meetings, she suggested that they become part of sustained solution rather than a foot-dragging part of the problem.

Holaday supervised a major upgrade of the sewage-treatment plant in Newburyport. She also was verbal about urging officials from Lowell, Lawrence, Haverhill, and Manchester, N.H., to spend more money and time to upgrade their treatment plants. Holaday, in her tenure in City Hall, was wont to complain, "We're at the end of the line in Newburyport. Will you upriver communities please improve your plants, so that the boating, fishing and viewing we all love will still be sustainable?" Upgrading is very expensive. Few candidates running for office in Lawrence or Haverhill would lead with a platform of cleaning the river, because it would be followed by voters saying, "We don't want increases to our sewer and water bills."

Above: Diana DiZoglio, former state senator from Methuen, has been a leader in the attempts to clean the Merrimack.

Left: This sculpture in Lowell pays homage to women who have worked in factories, homes, and environmental organizations along the Merrimack.

Going back more than a century, Ellen Swallow Richards was part of a state-appointed team brought in to determine if the Merrimack drinking water was leading the typhoid deaths of youngsters in Lawrence. In the 1880s, most officials said the drinking water in Lawrence was fine. It wasn't. Sickness and deaths resulted.

She and others were able to develop a more effective method to transform river water into safe drinking water. A new system was put into place, and these improved methods were adapted in other parts of the country. Today, almost 600,000 residents (though not in Newburyport) still get their drinking water from the Merrimack. That should be reason No. 1 that all communities should strive for a cleaner river, despite the cost. In 2023, many groups are working for a cleaner Merrimack. Yet recent CSOs remind us that progress is slow. With DiZoglio and Holaday departing the scene, those who love the river have lost two energetic and effective advocates. U.S. Rep. Lori Trahan, who represents the Lowell area, is one of the few elected watchdogs left. Perhaps other voter-approved officials or career public servants will step forward in the next year to make a clean Merrimack a top priority.

The location where the Merrimack meets the Atlantic is narrow and shallow, with sand bars that make navigation difficult.

17

Tributaries Are Important Components of the Merrimack

The 117-mile Merrimack River has about seventy tributaries and streams that eventually flow into the waterway. Environmental experts say keeping the tributaries clean and flowing freely are key elements of a healthy river. These excerpts come from Wikipedia.[1]

The Artichoke River is a 1.2-mile tributary in Essex County and flows generally north, marking the boundary between West Newbury and Newburyport. The Upper and Lower Artichoke reservoirs are impoundments of the river that act as a water source for nearby towns. Despite the short length of the river, there are three dams along its course—the Emory Lane Dam, the Lower Artichoke Dam, and the Upper Artichoke Dam. The river is named for the Jerusalem Artichoke, which had been harvested nearby by Native Americans and early settlers.

The Assabet River is a 34.4-mile-long river located about 20 miles west of Boston. The Assabet rises from a swampy area known as the Assabet Reservoir in Westborough and flows northeast before merging with the Sudbury River at Egg Rock in Concord to become the Concord River. As the Concord River is a tributary of the Merrimack River, it and the Assabet and Sudbury rivers are part of the larger Merrimack River watershed.

Baboosic Brook is a 12.7-mile-long stream, located in southern New Hampshire. It is a tributary of the Souhegan River, which flows to the Merrimack. Baboosic Brook begins at the outlet of Baboosic Lake in the town of Amherst. The brook takes a winding course (east- and southward flow predominating) through the towns of Amherst, Bedford, and Merrimac before ending at the Souhegan River near its outlet to the Merrimack River. Tributaries include Joe English Brook, Pulpit Brook, McQuade Brook, and Riddle Brook, all entering from the north.

The Back River is a 6.5-mile-long river in New Hampshire and Massachusetts. It is a tributary to the Powwow River, part of the Merrimack River watershed. Approximately 3 miles of the river are in New Hampshire, with the remaining 3.5 miles in Massachusetts. Prior to European settlement in the early seventeenth century, Native Americans of the Pennacook tribe lived in the area and used both the Back River and parent Powwow River for transportation and fishing. The native population was essentially destroyed by the 1617–19 epidemic in the area. In the 1950s, the Clarks Pond Dam was built in Amesbury, creating the pond of that name. Since the pond's creation, it has been degraded by residential building in the area and was considered "threatened" in a 2013 report, by residential run-off and silt deposits. The Back River rises in Kensington, N.H., and flows southeast, almost immediately entering the town of South Hampton. The river turns south and enters Massachusetts in Amesbury, joining the Powwow River at tidewater just downstream from the city's center at the falls of the Powwow.

The Baker River, or *Asquamchumauke* (an Abenaki word meaning "salmon spawning place"), is a 36.4-mile-long river in the White mountains of New Hampshire. The river traverses the towns of Warren, Wentworth, and Rumney. It is part of the Merrimack River Watershed. The Baker River's name recalls Lt. Thomas Baker (1682–1753), whose company of 34 scouts from Northhampton, Mass., passed down the river's valley in 1712 and destroyed a Pemigewasset Indian village. On the 1835 Thomas Bradford map of New Hampshire, the river is shown as "Bakers" River, originating on "Mooshillock Mtn."

Bear Brook is a 10-mile-long stream located in central New Hampshire. It is a tributary of the Suncook River, part of the Merrimack River. Its entire course is within Bear Brook State Park. Bear Brook begins at the outlet of Hall Mountain Marsh near the four-corner intersection of the towns of Allenstown, Deerfield, Candia, and Hooksett. The brook descends to the north, through Deerfield, then turns west and reenters Allenstown. Nearing Deerfield Road, the brook is impounded by Catamount Pond, with a state park beach and picnic area. The brook flows northwest from the pond and reaches the Suncook River in less than a mile.

Beards Brook or Beard Brook is a 12.5-mile-long stream, located in southern New Hampshire. It is a tributary of the North Branch of the Contoocook River, part of the Merrimack River watershed. Beards Brook begins at the outlet of Island Pond in the town of Washington. It descends rapidly northeast to the village of East Washington, then turns south and enters Hillsborough. A significant tributary is Shedd Brook, entering from the west in Hillsborough. Beards Brook joins the North Branch of the Contoocook near Hillsborough village, just upstream of the Contoocook River.

Beaver Brook is a 30.7-mile-long river located in both states. It is a tributary of the Merrimack River. Beaver Brook rises in Chester, N.H., and flows south into Derry passing through Harantis Lake, Adams Pond, and Beaver Lake. Continuing south, the brook forms the boundary between Londonderry and Windham, and then flows through Pelham. The brook crosses the state line into Dracut, Mass., and reaches the Merrimack in the city of Lowell. Most of the brook's course is through gently hilly terrain that is rapidly being converted into suburban land use.

The Beebe River is a 16.7-mile-long waterway located in the White Mountains of New Hampshire. It is tributary of the Pemisgewasset River, part of the Merrimack River watershed. The Beebe River begins at Black Mountain Pond on the southern slopes of Sandwich Mountain, a summit in the southern White Mountains, in the town of Sandwich. The river drops off the mountain to the south, then turns west to travel through Sandwich Notch, staying in a wooded valley and entering the town of Campton. The valley broadens as the river approaches the village of Campton Hollow, where the river reaches New Hampshire Route 175. and drops over some small waterfalls. The river passes by the old industrial community of Beebe River and reaches the Pemigewasset River next to Interstate 93.

A bridge in Franconia Notch, part of the Pemi River tributary in New Hampshire. (*Wikipedia photo*)

The Big River is a 14.9-mile-long river located in central New Hampshire. It is a tributary of the Suncook River, part of the Merrimack River. Headwaters of the Big River rise on high ground in the southern corners of Alton and New Durham, N.H. The river flows southeast into Strafford, then, running up against the Blue Hills Range, the river reverses course, turning west into Barnstead, where it meets the Suncook River in the village of Center Barnstable.

Black Brook is an 11.4-mile-long stream located in southern New Hampshire. Black Brook begins at the outlet of Kimball Pond in Dunbarton. The brook travels southeast into Goffstown and then Manchester, joining the Merrimack just upstream from Amoskeag Falls.

The Blackwater River is a 37.5-mile-long waterway located in central New Hampshire. It is a tributary of the Contoocook River, part of the Merrimack River watershed. The Blackwater River is formed at Cilleyville, a village in the western part of the town of Andover, by the junction of two branch streams. Cascade Brook, the western branch, begins at Cascade Marsh in the northeast part of Sutton, and flows northeast to Wilmot Flat, where it is joined by the outlet of Pleasant Lake of New London before continuing east to Cilleyville. Frazier Brook, the northern stream branch, rises just south of Danbury village and flows south parallel to Route 4, passing South Danbury, flowing through Eagle Pond in Wilmot and then through Bog Pond below West Andover, joining Cascade Brook just south of the outlet of Bog Pond. Kimpton Brook (formerly known as Quickwater Brook) flowing easterly through the village of Wilmot Center, is the primary tributary of Eagle Pond. From its start at Cilleyville, the Blackwater River flows east through the town of Andover, passing the village of Potter Place. Beyond Andover village, the river continues to wind its way east, eventually turning south near the Blackwater Bays and dropping over rapids through the village of West Salisbury to the impoundment area of the Blackwater Dam, in the town of Webster. Below the reservoir dam, the Blackwater encounters a short, intense whitewater stretch.

The Cockermouth River is a 9.5-mile-long stream located in central New Hampshire. It is the longest tributary of Newfound Lake, part of the Pemigewasset River and ultimately Merrimack River watersheds. The river takes its name from the "Cockermouth Grant," an early name for a portion of the town of Hebron. The river begins in Province Road State Forest near the western boundary of Groton, N.H., and proceeds southeast across the entire town of Groton. The river is closely paralleled by Sculptured Rocks Road, a very rough dirt road that gradually becomes more passable to automobiles as it proceeds downstream. The river passes through Sculptered Rocks Natural Area, a series of narrow, sharply carved rock formations that are a popular local swimming hole, then enters a broader valley as it passes the village center of Groton. Continuing east, the Cockermouth River enters the town of Hebron and flows into Newfound Lake near the lake's northern end.

The Nashua River meets the Merrimack River in Nashua, N.H.

Cohas Brook is a 16.5-mile-long river located in southern New Hampshire. Cohas Brook rises in Auburn, N.H., north of Calef Pond. The brook follows a winding course westward to the Merrimack River in Manchester. In Manchester, it picks up the outlet of Massabesic Lake, the water supply for the city. This lower portion was formerly known as the "Coos River." Much of the brook's course is quite close to intense suburban development, including Interstate routes 93 and 293, the South Willow Street commercial corridor, and Manchester-Boston Regional Airport.

The Concord River is a 16.3-mile-long tributary. The river drains a small rural and suburban region northwest of Boston. One of the most famous small rivers in U.S. history, it was the scene of an important early battle of the American Revolutionary War and was the subject of a famous nineteenth-century book by Henry David Thoreau.

The Contoocook River is a 71-mile-long river in New Hampshire. It flows from Contoocook Lake on the Jaffrey–Rindge border to Penacook (just north of Concord) where it empties into the Merrimack. It is one of only a few rivers in New Hampshire that flow in a predominantly northward direction. Residents and tourists have made the Contoocook popular for fishing and whitewater boating. The name "*Contoocook*" came from the Pennacook tribe of Native Americans and perhaps means "place of the river near pines."

The East Branch of the Baker River is a 3.1-mile-long waterway in western New Hampshire. It is a tributary of the Baker River, part of the Pemigewasset River and the Merrimack River and Merrimack River watersheds. The river rises on the southernmost slopes of Mount Moosilauke in the town of Woodstock. Flowing south, it quickly enters the town of Warren and crosses twice under Route 118 before joining the main stem of the Baker.

The East Branch of the Pemigewasset River is a 15.8-mile-long river located in the White Mountains of New Hampshire. It is a tributary of the Pemigewasset River, part of the Merrimack River watershed. The East Branch is a longer and larger river than the river that it flows into, but it is named a branch of the main stem because its source lies deep in the Pemigewasset Wilderness, of the White Mountains, while the main Pemigewasset River flows directly from Franconia Notch, a major pass through the mountains.

The Fowler River is a 6.1-mile-long waterway located in central New Hampshire. It is an inflow to Newfound Lake, part of the Pemigewasset and Merrimack River watersheds. Below Bog Brook, the Fowler River is subject to the New Hampshire Comprehensive Shoreland Protection Act. The primary tributary of the river is Clark Brook, which rises south of Mount Cardigan in the town of Alexandria and drops over Welton Falls. Chesley Brook joins from the north, at which point the stream valley widens and begins to support small agricultural operations. The brook's name changes to "Fowler River" when Brock Brook joins from the right at the first crossing of Fowler River Road. The river flows southeast to a junction with Bog Brook, where it turns north and flows 1 mile to Newfound Lake.

Frazier Brook is a 7.7-mile-long stream in central New Hampshire, via the Blackwater and Contocook rivers, and it is part of Merrimack River Watershed. It is subject to the New Hampshire Comprehensive Shoreland Protection Act. Frazier Brook begins in Danbury, New Hampshire, just south of the town center, and flows south through the town of Wilmot into Andover. Eagle Pond and Bog Pond interrupt the brook's flow. Shortly below Bog Pond, the brook reaches the Blackwater River at the village of Cilleyville. Frazier Brook is paralleled for most of its length by U.S. Route 4.

The Gunstock River is a 6.4-mile-long river in the Lakes Region of central New Hampshire. It is a tributary of Lake Winnipesaukee, part of the Merrimack River watershed. The Gunstock River is entirely within the town of Gilford. It rises in the southern part of town, west of Piper Mountain, and flows north, collecting streamflow from the west side of the Belknap Range. The river flows through a wide valley in the center of Gilford, passing the town's middle and high schools, then drops through a steep ravine before reaching flat ground near Lake Winnipesaukee. The river enters the lake at Sanders Bay, near the junction of Routes 11 and 11B.

The Lane River is an 8.5-mile-long stream in central New Hampshire. It is a tributary of the Warner River, part of the Contoocook River and ultimately the Merrimack River watershed. The Lane River begins at the outlet of Kezar Lake in the village of North Sutton. The river flows south through a broad wetland, incorporating the outflow of Gile Pond, then suddenly drops 140 feet to enter the village of Sutton. The river continues southeast through more wetlands and past the village of South Sutton, then becomes more rapid as it descends to the Warner River at the Sutton town line.

The Little River is a 4.9-mile-long waterway, located in central New Hampshire. Its outflow travels via the Big River, Suncook River and the Merrimack River, to the Gulf of Maine. The Little River begins on the west side of the Blue Hills Range in Strafford, N.H., It flows northwest, gaining the outlet of the Willey Ponds, and joins the Big River just north of the village of South Barnstead.

The Little River (same name, different location) is a 12.9-mile-long river in New Hampshire and Massachusetts. It is a tributary of the Merrimack River. The Little River rises in Kingston, N.H. It flows south through Plaistow, and enters the city of Haverhill, Mass., where it joins the Merrimack River. Most of the Little River's course is marked by suburban and urban development.

Little Massabesic Brook and Sucker Brook form a 1.9-mile-long stream located in southern New Hampshire. Despite the streams' short length, they are subject to the New Hampshire Comprehensive Shoreland Protection Act, because of their fourth-order stream status (indicating a high number of upstream tributary set). Little Massabesic Brook begins at the outlet of Little Massabesic Lake in Auburn, N.H., and flows west to Clark Pond Brook. At this juncture, the stream changes its name to Sucker Brook and flows south, past the village proper of Auburn, and enters Massabesic Lake.

The Little Suncook River is a 4-mile-long river in central New Hampshire. It is a tributary of the Suncook River, part of the Merrimack River watershed. The Little Suncook begins at the outlet of Northwood Lake, in the town of Epsom. Flowing west, it passes through Bixby Pond (also known as Cass Pond), passes the villages of Epsom and Gossville, and joins the Suncook River near the Epsom Traffic Circle. U.S. Route 4 parallels the Little Suncook for the river's entire length.

The Lost River is a 4-mile-long stream in the White Mountains of New Hampshire. It is a tributary of the Moosilauke Brook, part of the Pemigewasset River watershed, leading to the Merrimack River. As it flows through the Kinsman Nother, it passes through Lost River Gorge, an area where enormous boulders falling off the flanking walls of the notch at the close of the last Ice Age have covered the river, creating a network of boulder caves. The gorge is owned by the Society for the Protection of

New Hampshire Forests and is operated as a tourist attraction, with trails and ladders accessing many of the caves.

The Mad River is a 17.9-mile-long river in the White Mountains of New Hampshire. It is a tributary of the Pemigewasset River, part of the Merrimack River watershed. After winding through the Waterville Valley Resort community, the Mad River proceeds southwest over continuous boulder-strewn rapids into a corner of the town of Thornton, eventually settling out in Campton Pond in the town of Campton. Passing over a small hydroelectric dam at Campton Upper Village, the river descends over some small waterfalls and enters the floodplain of the Pemigewasset River, which it joins near Interstate 93. For most of the river's length below Waterville Valley, it is paralleled by New Hampshire Route 49.

The Melvin River is an 8.1-mile-long river in the Lakes River of central New Hampshire. It is a tributary of Lake Winnipesaukee, part of the Merrimack River watershed. The Melvin River lies entirely within the town of Tuftonboro. The river reaches Lake Winnipesaukee at Melvin Village.

The Merrymeeting River is a 10-mile-long river in central New Hampshire. The river begins at the outlet of Merrymeeting Lake in the town of New Durham. The river flows south through a chain of ponds to the village proper of New Durham. The river enters Merrymeeting Marsh and turns sharply to the northwest, the course it will take the rest of the way to its end. The river crosses a small dam at Alton and reaches Lake Winnipesaukee at the community of Alton Bay, the southernmost point on the lake.

The Middle Branch of the Piscataquog River is a 10.6-mile-long river in southern New Hampshire. It is a tributary of the South Branch Piscataquog River. The Middle Branch begins at the outlet of Haunted Lake in the eastern part of Francestown. The river travels east-northeast through the town of New Boston, entering Ware, where it turns abruptly south to reenter New Boston.

Moosilauke Brook is a 3.2-mile-long stream in the White Mountains of New Hampshire. It is the downstream continuation of the Lost River and is a tributary of the Pemigewasset River. Moosilauke Brook begins in the eastern part of Kinsman Notch, where the Lost River, flowing out of the center of the notch, joins Jackman Brook entering from the south. Moosilauke Brook runs northeast, passing through the granite gorge of Agassiz Basin, and joining the Pemigewasset River in the village of North Woodstock. New Hampshire Route 112 follows Moosilauke Brook for its entire course.

The Nashua River, 37.5 miles long, is a tributary of the Merrimack River in Massachusetts and New Hampshire. The Nashua River watershed occupies a major portion of north-central Massachusetts and a much smaller portion of southern New Hampshire. The North Nashua River rises west of Fitchburg and Westminster. It flows about 30 miles generally southeast past Fitchburg, and joins the South Nashua River, shown on USGS topographic maps as the main stem of the Nashua River, about 5 miles below its issuance from the Wachusett Reservoir.

The Newfound River is a 3.2-mile-long river in central New Hampshire. It is a tributary of the Pemigewasset River. The river drops rapidly through the town of Bristol, passing over several hydroelectric dams before reaching the Pemigewasset. Major tributaries of the Newfound River (via Newfound Lake) are the Fowler River and the Cockermouth River.

The Nissitissit River is a 10.5-mile-long river in southern New Hampshire and northern Massachusetts. It is tributary of the Nashua River. The Nissitissit River begins at the outlet of Potanipo Pond, in the town of Brookline, N.H. It flows southeast at a very mild gradient, crossing the southwest corner of Hollis, N.H., before entering Massachusetts, where it joins the Nashua River in the town of Pepperell.

The North Branch of the Contoocook River (officially the North Branch River) is a 16.8-mile-long river in southwestern New Hampshire. The North Branch begins in a highland region of lakes, swamps, and intricate stream networks in the town of Stoddard, N.H. From Franklin Pierce Lake, the North Branch consists of a stairstep-like series of flatwater and wetland sections interspersed with sections of whitewater that are popular among New England kayakers. New Hampshire Route 9 follows the North Branch for most of the river's length.

Nubanusit Brook is a 14.3-mile-long stream in southern New Hampshire. The brook begins at the outlet of Nubanusit Lake in Nelson. Nubanusit Brook was important to the establishment and development of Harrisville and Peterborough because many dams were built along it to provide water power to mills. These included substantial textile mills in Harrisville, West Peterborough, and Peterborough, as well as smaller mills along the brook's course.

The Pemigewasset River known locally as "The Pemi," is a river in New Hampshire. It is 65 miles in length and (with its tributaries) drains approximately 1,021 square miles. The name "Pemigewasset" comes from the Abenaki word meaning "where side (entering) current is." The Pemigewasset originates at Profile Lake in the town of Franconia. It flows south through the White Mountains and merges with the Winnipesaukee River to form the Merrimack River in Franklin.

Pennichuck Brook is one of the tributaries of the Merrimack. Its watershed is 31 square miles and is one of the 14 sub-watersheds of the Merrimack River. It passes through Nashua and Merrimack, N.H., and serves as the public water supply for greater Nashua.

The Piscataquog River is a 34.7-mile-long river in southern New Hampshire. The Piscataquog River begins at the outlet of Deering Reservoir in Deering, N.H. The river takes a winding course north, then east, then south, then east again to reach the Merrimack River in Manchester. Going south from Goffstown, there are two small reservoirs and several additional dams, each constructed for hydroelectric power or older industrial development. In west Manchester, the Piscataquog passes under the Nazaire Biron Bridge and reaches the Merrimack River just upstream of the Queen City Bridge.

The Powwow River is a 22.8-mile-long river located in New Hampshire and Massachusetts. It is a one of the larger Massachusetts tributaries of the Merrimack. The Powwow River rises in the center of Danville, N.H. The river eventually turns southeast and enters South Hampton, NH., where it flows into Tuxbury Pond and crosses into Amesbury, Mass. Below the outlet of the pond, the river winds easterly along the state line before entering Massachusetts for good at Lake Gardner. The river then flows through the center of Amesbury, where it drops 90 feet over falls and rapids before reaching the Merrimack River.

Purgatory Brook is a 5.8-mile-long tributary of the Souhegan River in southern New Hampshire. It rises in a marshy area on the border of Lyndeborough and Mont Vernon. and flows south over three small waterfalls, intersecting the Souhegan in Milford. For much of its length, it constitutes the border between Lyndeborough and Mont Vernon. The northernmost cascade, Upper Purgatory Falls, attracted many visitors in the late nineteenth and early twentieth century when Mont Vernon was home to several hotels that drew summer visitors from Boston. Today, the upper falls can be reached on the Mont Vernon side by four-wheel drive vehicles, and on the Lyndeborough side by a short walk from a town-maintained road. The lowest waterfall can only be reached by a short hiking trail from a parking lot, which has been closed due to overcrowding spurred by the COVID-19 pandemic. The middle waterfall can be reached by a public trail that runs the length of the brook.

The Quinapoxet River is part of the Nashua River watershed in northern Massachusetts. It is part of the Massachusetts Water Resources Authority water system supplying drinking water to the greater Boston area. The Quinapoxet Dam in Holden impounds 1.1 million gallons in the Quinapoxet Reservoir, a Worcester drinking water supply.

The Red Hill River is a 6.5-mile-long river central New Hampshire. It is a tributary of Lake Winnipesaukee, part of the Merrimack River watershed. The Red Hill River begins in the town of Sandwich, N.H., at the outlet of Little Pond Red Hill Pond, just east of the village of Sandwich. The river passes through Garland Pond and drops in a short river segment past the hamlet of Moultonborough Falls to Lees Pond, the outlet of which leads almost directly into an arm of Moultonborough Bay on Lake Winnipesaukee.

The Powwow River runs through Amesbury, Mass., before reaching the Merrimack.

Salmon Brook is one of the six major tributaries of the Merrimack River in northeastern Massachusetts. Its watershed is 31 sq. miles and is one of the fourteen sub-watersheds of the Merrimack River. It passes through Dunstable, Mass., and Nashua, N.H.

The Shawsheen River is a 26.7-mile-long tributary of the Merrimack River in northeast Massachusetts. The river runs generally northward through the towns of Bedford, Billerica, Wilmington, Tewksbury, Andover, and Lawrence, where it joins the Merrimack. Like its parent, the river has played an important role in the development of the area, including industrial development, with many mills built to take advantage of the river's power. Today there are trails and parks located along several sections of the river, and a preservation effort is carried out by the Shawsheen River Watershed Association. In June 2001, the Merrimack River Watershed Council determined that the Shawsheen River failed to meet water quality standards. This situation was largely attributed to stormwater runoff via town, private and state storm drain systems. As a result of increased pollutants, major portions of the Shawsheen River are now listed as impaired waters. The removal of the Marland Place Dam (originally built in the 1700s) and Balmoral Dam (originally built in the 1920s) allowed alewife and blueback herring to spawn upstream to the Ballardvale Dam in spring 2017, for the first time in over 200 years.

Shedd Brook is an 11.3-mile-long stream located in southern New Hampshire. It is a tributary of Beards Brook, part of the Contoocook River and the Merrimack River. Shedd Brook begins at the north outlet of Highland Lake in Washington, N.H. The brook flows east, entering Hillsborough. Hillsborough Upper Village is located where Black Pond Brook descends over falls to join Shedd Brook, which ends two miles downstream at Beards Brook. New Hampshire Route 31 follows Shedd Brook in Washington and Windsor.

The Smith River is a 25-mile-long waterway located in central New Hampshire. It is a tributary of the Pemigewasset River, part of the Merrimack River watershed. The Smith River begins at the outlet of Tewksbury Pond in Grafton, N.H. Passing under the New Hampshire Route 3A bridge at the Bristol Hill town line, the Smith River drops over Profile Falls and arrives at the Pemigewasset River.

The Soucook River is a 29.2-mile-long river in central New Hampshire. It is a tributary of the Merrimack River. The river flows south through gently rolling terrain, soon entering Loudon and passing near the New Hampshire Motor Speedway. The river passes through the village proper of Loudon, crossing a small dam, and continues south along a more suburban corridor on the outskirts of Concord. The river forms the boundary between Concord and Pembroke and ends at the Merrimack River downstream from Garvins Falls. There are extensive sand and gravel deposits filling the Soucook River valley, which has led to the creation of several large excavation operations close to the river. New Hampshire Route 106 parallels the river throughout its course, crossing the river four times.

The Souhegan River is a tributary of the Merrimack. It is 33.8 miles with a drainage area of 171 square miles flowing north and east through southern New Hampshire to the Merrimack River. The river is used for water supplies, a small amount of hydopower and recreation. There are twenty-eight threatened or endangered species sharing the watershed with 35,000 people. It is part of the New Hampshire Rivers Management

Protection Program. It was one of two rivers studied by the New Hampshire Department of Environmental Services to reach data and recommendations about allowable "instream flow."

The South Branch of the Baker River is a 15.6-mile-long river located in western New Hampshire. It is a tributary of the Baker River, part of the Pemigewasset River and the Merrimack River watersheds.

The South Branch of the Piscataquog River is a 20.5-mile-long river located in southern New Hampshire. It is a tributary of the Piscatagoug River, part of the Merrimack River watershed. For most of its route, the South Branch passes through rolling, hilly country, occasionally dropping over small waterfalls. New Hampshire Route 13 follows the river closely from New Boston to Goffstown.

The South Branch of the Souhegan River is a 5.8-mile-long river in northern Massachusetts and southern New Hampshire. It is a tributary of the Souhegan River, which flows to the Merrimack. The South Branch begins near Mount Watatic at the outlet of Stodge Meadow Pond in the town of Ashburnam, Mass and flows north through a chain of small lakes (Marble Pond, Ward Pond, and Watatic Pond) before turning northeast into the town of Ashby, Mass. North of Ashby, the river enters New Ipswich, N.H., passes through a small flood control reservoir, and joins the West Branch to form the Souhegan River, just north of the intersection known as "Gibson Four Corners."

The Spicket River is a 17.7-mile-long river located in New Hampshire and Massachusetts. The Spicket flows south into Salem, N.H., passing through the Arlington Mill Reservoir. The river continues through Salem, encountering suburban development, and enters the city of Methuen, Mass., where it drops nearly 100 feet in elevation over a series of dams on its way to the Merrimack River in Lawrence.

The Squam River is a 3.6-mile-long river located in central New Hampshire. The river is the outlet of Squam Lake, the second-largest lake in New Hampshire, and it is a tributary of the Pemi River, of which itself is a tributary of the Merrimack. The Squam River first appears as a narrow channel in Holderness, N.H., between Squam Lake and Little Squam Lake. The two lakes have the same elevation, due to a dam below the outlet to Little Squam, so the river in Holderness village is not free flowing. Below Little Squam Lake the river proceeds south for over a mile before reaching the dam which controls the two lakes' water level. Below this point, the river quickly reaches the backwater from a mill dam in the town of Ashland. In Ashland, the river drops 50 feet, sufficient to provide hydropower for numerous industries when the town originally grew in the nineteenth century. Below the center of town, the river wanders southeast past the Ashland sewage treatment plant before entering the Pemigewasset River in the northwest corner of the town of New Hampton.

The Squannacook River is a 16.4-mile-long river in northern Massachusetts. The river rises within West Townsend, Mass., at the juncture of Walker Brook, Locke Brook, and Willard Brook. Walker and Locke Brooks rise within Greenwille, New Ipswich and Mason, N.H., through Townsend and West Groton, Mass., and joins the Nashua River in wetlands just east of Woodsville. The river is dammed three times in Townsend and twice in West Groton. Its watershed covers 73 square miles of which 18 percent is permanently protected. It has been designated an Outstanding Resource Water. There has been a conversion of one of the former mills on the Groton portion of the river.

The Stillwater River is part of the Nashua River watershed. This river is part of the Massachusetts Water Resources Authority system that supplies drinking water to the greater Boston area. The Stillwater River rises in Princeton, Mass., watershed tops at Wachusett Mountain, the highest feature in the area. Water flowing east from this high ground feeds the Nashua River Watershed, and water flowing west feeds the Ware River or the Millers River, both heading toward the Connecticut River. The Stillwater and Quinapoxet rivers are the two major tributaries to the Wachusett Reservoir, which serves as the primary source of water for 2.5 million consumers in 43 communities of central and eastern Massachusetts. The U.S. Geological Survey in cooperation with the Massachusetts Department of Conservation and Recreation, operates streamflow monitoring gages near the mouths of both rivers.

Stony Brook is a 10.6-mile-long river located in southern New Hampshire. It is a tributary of the Souhegan River, which flows to the Merrimack. Stony Brook rises in the town of Lyndeborough, N.H., in a valley between Lyndeborough Mountain to the north and Winn Mountain to the south. It flows west into the town of Greenfield, then turns southeast and reenters Lyndeborough, continuing to the Souhegan in the mill town of Wilton.

The Sudbury River is a 32.7-mile-long tributary of the Concord River in Massachusetts. Originating in the Cedar Swamp in Westborough, Mass. near the boundary with Hopkinton, the Sudbury River meanders generally northeast, through Fairhaven Bay, and to its confluence with the Assabet River at Egg Rock in Concord, Mass. to form the Concord River. It has a 162-square-mile drainage area. In 1999, nearly 17 miles of the river were "recognized for their outstanding ecology, history, scenery, recreation values, and place in American literature," by being designated as a part of the National Wild and Scenic Rivers System. Mercury contamination was discovered in the 1970s from the Nyanza plant in Ashland. The EPA subsequently listed the town as a toxic site and led a cleanup effort to repair the damage. It is still recommended that fish caught downriver not be eaten.

The Suncook River is a 35.7-mile-long river in central New Hampshire. On May 16, 2006, the Suncook River absorbed the highest rainfall amounts in at least seventy years. More than 8 inches dropped by a low-pressure system in three days on Concord, N.H. rose to flood level, and backed up behind an old mill dam, which produced a shallowly-sloping pool that overtopped a sand and gravel quarry, connected with a downstream section of channel, and cut a new shorter channel at 25–50 meters per hour in the town of Epsom. Two previous channels, around Bear Island, were left dry. The new river course, approximately a mile long, is the largest channel change in a river in New Hampshire since systematic topographic mapping began in the state in the early twentieth century.

The Tioga River is a 12.8-mile-long river located in the Lakes Region of central New Hampshire. The Tioga River rises on the western slopes of the Belknap Mountains in Gilmanton, N.H. Flowing west, the river quickly enters the town of Belmont, where it spends most of its existence. The river passes through Badger Pond shortly before reaching the village proper of Belmont, which was sited along the Tioga River in the nineteenth century for its waterpower. New Hampshire Route 140 follows the general course of the river from Belmont village to the Winnipesaukee.

The Turkey River is a 6.1-mile-long stream located in southern New Hampshire. The source of the Turkey River is the outlet of Little Turkey Pond in Concord, N.H. The river travels southeast through the campus of St. Paul's School, winding through the outskirts of Concord, and entering Bow, before joining the Merrimack near the junction of Interstate 93 and Interstate 89.

The Warner River is a 20.3-mile-long river located in central New Hampshire. It is a tributary of the Contoocook River. The small river has a long whitewater section in western Warner, passing under the Waterloo Covered Bridge, next to an old railroad station, then reaches Interstate 89, after which the river flattens and meanders over gravel bars. A small waterfall at Davisville interrupts the flatwater, which resumes to the river's end, just north of the village of Contoocook, N.H.

The West Branch of the Mad River is a 3.2-mile-long stream located in the White Mountains of New Hampshire. It is a tributary of the Mad River. The West Branch joins the Mad River close to the center of the Waterville Valley resort.

The West Branch of the Souhegan River is a 3.1-mile-long river in southern New Hampshire. The West Branch is located entirely in the town of New Ipswich, N.H. It begins at the junction of Fox Brook and Pratt Pond Brook, southwest of the town center, and flows east through the settlement known as Smithville, ending at its junction with the South Branch of the Souhegan River north of Gibson Four Corners.

The West Branch of the Warner River is a 6.5-mile-long river in central New Hampshire. The West Branch rises in the southwest corner of Newbury, N.H., on the eastern slopes of Mount Sunapee. Flowing east, it quickly enters the town of Bradford, reaching the Warner River at the town center.

The Winnipesaukee River is a 10.5-mile-long river that connects Lake Winnipesaukee with the Pemi and Merrimack rivers in Franklin, N.H. The river has two distinct sections. The upstream section consists of a series of river courses connecting a chain of lakes, beginning with Lake Winnipesaukee. From the dam at the outlet of Lake Winnipesaukee in the Lakeport section of Laconia, the river almost immediately enters Opechee Bay. The river exits over a dam and drops through the center of Laconia, its banks lined by industrial buildings from the 19th century that were constructed to take advantage of the river's power. The 1-mile section through Laconia ends at Lake Winnisquam, the fourth-largest lake in New Hampshire. A 5-mile stretch across Winnisquam leads to the dam at the lake's outlet and a short descent to Silver Lake. The Winnipesaukee River joins the Pemigewasset River just downstream from the center of Franklin, forming the Merrimack River.

Part of the Turkey River in New Hampshire.

A winter stream in New Hampshire descends to the Merrimack.

18

Water Infrastructure Finance and Innovation Act (WIFIA) Has Made Billions Available to Clean the River

This article is excerpted from a trade magazine, *Treatment Plant Operator*. It was published in November 2021, and explains that new funding will be available to clean rivers and other waterways in coming years.

The U.S. House of Representatives recently passed the $1.2 trillion Infrastructure Investment and Jobs act, and President Joe Biden signed the bill into law to cement a major funding boost for the water/wastewater sector.

The Association of Metropolitan Water Agencies reports that the bill carries $48.4 billion over five years for drinking water and wastewater spending at EPA, including:

- $11.713 billion each to the Drinking Water and Clean Water State Revolving Funds, with states required to award precisely 49 percent of their share of these funds as grants or full principal forgiveness loans.
- $15 billion through the DWSRF to support lead service line replacement projects, again with 49 percent of funds required to be distributed by states as grants or principal forgiveness loans.
- A total of $10 billion to help drinking water and wastewater systems address emerging contaminants like per- and polyfluoroalkyl substances (PFAS), including $4 billion through the DWSRF as grants that would be available to drinking water systems of all sizes.

The bill also authorizes several new EPA programs, such as a new climate resilience program for drinking water systems that has been long championed by AMWA and a low-income water ratepayer assistance pilot program. However, those programs would not receive funding through the bill and would instead have to wait for dollars through subsequent appropriations legislation. Water Environment Federation President Jamie Eichenberger says the final passage by Congress of this infrastructure package will give the water sector the largest boost in federal funding for local water infrastructure it has received in decades.

A statement from the American Water Works Association said the group is grateful to the federal government for making water infrastructure a priority.

A pipe that collects surface water in Newburyport dumps the foul mix into the Merrimack near the city's boardwalk.

A fish lift in Manchester, N.H., was designed to provide a route upriver.

> By reauthorizing the Water Infrastructure Finance and Innovation Act and doubling funding for the drinking water State Revolving Fund, the federal government is helping states and local water providers to spur on critical water projects. In addition, the $15 billion designated for lead service line replacement is a welcome down payment on what could be a $60 billion challenge.

National Association of Clean Water Agencies CEO Adam Krantz applauded the Biden Administration and leaders in both the House and Senate for working across party lines to pass the bill:

> Just as roads, bridges, and broadband contribute to vibrant communities, the public clean water sector is vital to America's public health and the environment. This legislation takes strides to help provide all households with clean and safe water services at an affordable cost. NACWA's members look forward to working with stakeholders at all levels of government to implement this legislation.

Patricia Sinicropi, executive director of the WateReuse Association, also offered a statement in support of the bill:

> Communities across the country are incorporating water reuse into their water management strategies as a proven method for ensuring a safe, reliable, locally controlled water supply—essential for livable communities with healthy environments, robust economies and a high quality of life ... With enactment of the bi-partisan infrastructure investment package, Congress and the Administration recognize the essential role water recycling is playing in helping communities confront the impacts of climate change and build more resilient and sustainable water resources for their communities. This is an important day for water in the U.S.

The following is a general guide to EPA funding, included here to inform both professionals and activists. The source is the EPA website. Administered by the states, the State Revolving Funds have the potential to support mitigation or post-disaster recovery and rebuilding projects.

Drinking Water State Revolving Funds

Description: The Drinking Water State Revolving Fund (DWSRF) provides below-market rate loans to fund infrastructure improvements to water systems to protect public health and ensure compliance with the Safe Drinking Water Act. These projects may include the installation, upgrade, and replacement of treatment facilities, finished water storage facilities, and transmission and distribution systems. Projects to consolidate water supplies may also be eligible. Dams and reservoirs are generally ineligible. Many states offer funding for disaster preparedness and recovery. DWSRF assistance can be used to purchase and construct resiliency- and recovery-related infrastructure improvements such as backup generators, physical flood barriers, redundant equipment and infrastructure, telemetry systems for remote operation, and saltwater-resistant equipment. Existing facilities can be modified or relocated; examples include moving a treatment plant out of the floodplain or deepening existing wells. Equipment can be physically hardened against hazards by waterproofing electrical components, sealing structures to prevent floodwater penetration, and adding wind-resistant features.

Many states offer DWSRF technical assistance and trainings for water utilities to bolster resiliency. This assistance helps water systems plan for and adapt to extreme weather, prepare for emergencies and disasters, and join Water/Wastewater Agency Response Networks (WARNs).

Eligibility: Project eligibility varies by state. Both publicly and privately-owned community water systems and non-profit, non-community water systems are eligible for funding.

Type and Cost Share: State DWSRF program assistance is typically in the form of low-interest loans. These loans range from zero percent to market rate. Utilities repay these loans over a period of up to 30 years. Terms can be up to 40 years for systems designated by the state as "disadvantaged." Some states offer additional subsidization, such as grants, principal forgiveness, and negative interest rate loans to these disadvantaged systems. Technical assistance and training activities for water systems is also available in most states.

Application: Application requirements vary by state. Water systems should contact their state program at the link below.

Clean Water State Revolving Funds

Description: The Clean Water State Revolving Fund (CWSRF) provides below-market rate loans for a wide range of water quality infrastructure projects, including publicly owned wastewater collection and treatment systems, stormwater management, nonpoint source pollution control, decentralized wastewater treatment, water reuse, and estuary management projects. Through the Green Project Reserve, the CWSRFs target critical green infrastructure, water and energy efficiency improvements, and other environmentally innovative activities. Many states offer financing for disaster preparedness and recovery. CWSRF assistance can be used to purchase and construct resiliency- and recovery-related infrastructure improvements such as backup generators, physical flood barriers, redundant equipment and infrastructure, telemetry systems for remote operation, and saltwater-resistant equipment. Existing facilities can be modified or relocated, such as moving a treatment plant out of the floodplain. Equipment can be physically hardened against hazards by waterproofing electrical components, sealing structures to prevent floodwater penetration, and adding wind-resistant features.

Eligibility: Project eligibility varies by state. Eligible loan recipients include, but are not limited to, municipalities, individuals, citizens' groups, and nonprofit organizations.

Type and Cost Share: CWSRF assistance is typically in the form of low-interest loans. These loans range from zero percent to market rate over a period of up to 30 years. Some states offer additional subsidization, such as grants, principal forgiveness, and negative interest rate loans.

Application: Application requirements vary by state. For more information, contact the appropriate state program.

Stripers are abundant in the lower Merrimack when the river is clean.

The river in winter is a destination for photographers. This scene is from Amesbury. (*Photo by Bryan Eaton*)

Description: The WIFIA program accelerates investment in our nation's water infrastructure by providing long-term, low-cost supplemental loans for regionally and nationally significant water and wastewater infrastructure projects. The WIFIA program can fund development and implementation activities for eligible projects:

- Wastewater conveyance and treatment projects that are eligible for the Clean Water SRF
- Drinking water treatment and distribution projects that are eligible for the Drinking Water SRF
- Enhanced energy efficiency projects at drinking water and wastewater facilities
- Brackish or seawater desalination, aquifer recharge, alternative water supply, and water recycling projects
- Drought prevention, reduction, or mitigation projects
- Acquisition of property if integral to a project or would mitigate environmental impact of a project
- Combination of projects secured by a common security pledge or submitted under one application by an SRF program.
- WIFIA works separately from, but in coordination with, the SRF programs to provide subsidized financing for large dollar-value projects.

Eligibility*:* Utilities operated by local, state, tribal, and federal government entities.

Type and Cost Share: The WIFIA program offers loans with low, fixed interest rates and flexible financial terms.

More information can be obtained at the website of the Water Infrastructure Finance and Innovation Act: epa.gov/wifia

19

Epilogue: Now is the Time to Obtain Federal Funding

In the spring of 2023, a curious disconnect existed between water-quality professionals who supervise the Merrimack River and consumers who fish, boat, and walk along the waterway.

Professionals considered the Merrimack to be much improved, and in pretty good shape. "The Merrimack is the cleanest it's been since the Clean Water Act was passed in 1972," said Fred McNeill, the director of the Manchester, N.H., water-treatment facility. He has been quoted extensively earlier in this book.

McNeill added, during an interview, "The commission was able to create a notification system, which requires sewage-treatment plant operators to inform the public of when they have had CSOs, and for how long. That is a big step forward."

But Paul Aziz, who runs a tour boat, the *Yankee Clipper*, out of Newburyport, had a different opinion. "I'm on the river almost every day in the summer," the captain said. "After it rains and the CSOs are coming downstream, the river can be very polluted."

Perhaps both observers are correct: The river is a lot cleaner, but more can be done. It also depends on where you are when making assessments. Those north of Manchester, N.H., have a largely unsullied river. But south of Manchester, the evidence of CSOs begins to dominate conversation. Newburyport has more than 1,500 pleasure vessels on moorings or in slips, and the community relies on clean water to maintain its reputation as a tourist destination.

Clam flats near Plum Island are sometimes open, and sometimes not. State officials monitor the water, and they maintain a clam-purification plant on the north end of Plum Island. That seems to tell the story. Sometimes water quality is good, with vessels in the river, and clammers on the flats. On other occasions, the flats are closed because of pollution, algae counts or both.

David Cash, executive director of the New England division of the Environmental Protection Agency, said he is pleased with the improvement of the Merrimack. "Over the years, things have really gotten better," said Cash, who I interviewed on January 31, 2023:

> Eagles have returned. There are many egrets in the area. The fishing can be very good. EPA is aware of problems in some riverside communities, and consent agreements exist

David Cash, head of the regional office of the Environmental Protection Agency in New England.

> with Manchester, Nashua, Lowell, Lawrence, and Haverhill. We know the problems and we work closely with those communities to improve.
>
> But it is complicated. And it is expensive. Yet we are making progress. The city of Manchester has begun an enormous improvement project that, in time, will cut the amount of CSOs significantly.

Sen. Bruce Tarr, a Gloucester Republican whose district includes Newburyport, is another veteran river-watcher. "In the last half-dozen years, we've seen an increase in communities' desire to clean up," said Tarr, who I interviewed on February 16, 2023:

> [Former] State Sen. Diana DiZoglio, former Newburyport mayor Donna Holaday and many others got together regularly to make improvements. Mayor Reardon in Newburyport is concerned. The Merrimack Valley Planning Commission has been working on this.

Some river-users say the waterway has improved in recent years but perhaps not fast enough. Dan Graovac, former chair of the Merrimack River Watershed Council, lives on Plum Island on the basin side. That means that detritus from toilet waste to hypodermic needles sometimes washes up from the river.

Above left: State Sen. Bruce Tarr, R-Gloucester, now represents Newburyport. He is a strong advocate for a cleaner waterway.

Above right: Paul Aziz, who captains tourist boats on the river, observes the waterway almost every day in summer.

Aziz, who has run a tourist boat for almost two decades on the Merrimack, said, "It's a major problem and I wish improvement could come faster."

Numerous "average" boaters and fishermen have decried the pollution after several days of rain. Most North Shore residents do not swim south of Manchester. And many will not eat fish taken from the Merrimack. All involved in the Merrimack's future are concerned about "forever chemicals," substances that enter the river from business and homes. Study of this phenomena continues, in part because 600,000 residents in a half-dozen communities get their drinking water from the Merrimack.

Congresswoman Lori Trahan, who represents the Lowell area, recently supported a new proposed rule by the EPA to half the production of an estimated 300 per-and-polyfluoroalkyl substances (PFAS) without prior approval. In February 2023, she said:

> This is great news for communities here in Massachusetts and across our nation that have been impacted by PFAS contaminations in their drinking water. By ending the

> wild west approach to PFAS chemical manufacturing, we can take necessary steps to clean up contaminated water sources and prevent future contaminations as well....
>
> Congress must act swiftly to pass the PFAS Action Act to bolster this new rule with the updated laws we need to protect families from these dangerous pollutants.

PFAS chemicals are manmade and have been used in common products such as firefighting foam, non-stick cookware, water-resistant clothing, cleaning products, paints and sealants, personal care products, and cosmetics. Manufacturers and distributors of products containing PFAS have known for decades about the dangers the chemicals pose to people's health but have done little about it. Despite warnings, some companies were dumping so much PFAS into waterways that they could not keep track of the exact amount. These "forever chemicals" have been discovered in the drinking water of more than 2,000 communities nationwide, including in public water sources in Massachusetts. Also, pipes and catch basins that dump surface water into the river can be improved.

There is one thing that many water-watchers agree on: Now is the time to seek federal money to improve facilities. "This is a big moment," said Cash. "Federal money is available. And a preference will be given to communities with black and brown communities. The thinking is that a bad environment affects low-income communities. So, this a very important time."

Much of the dissemination of money will be supervised by the EPA, and the state-revolving funds will be utilized. Officials say that local and state water-quality officials should consult appropriate authorities to learn how to apply for this money.

Swans are graceful denizens of the lower Merrimack. (*Dan Graovac photo*)

Endnotes

Introduction

1 "The EPA and the Bipartisan Infrastructure Law," fact sheet, from the website of the Environmental Protection Agency, p. 1, November 8, 2021.
2 Merrimack River Watershed Council, graphic with map, November 2022.

Chapter 1

1 Thoreau, H. D., *A Week on the Concord and Merrimack Rivers, 1849*, reprinted private edition.
2 Cash, D., director of the New England Office of the Environmental Protection Agency," interview, January 31, 2023.
3 Merrimack River Watershed Council, newsletter, fall 2022.

Chapter 3

1 Alliance of Climate and Environmental Stewards, Merrimack River User Survey, Newburyport, 2022.

Chapter 5

1 This essay by Fred McNeill, one of the region's most knowledgeable clean-water professionals, was published in professional journals in the summer of 2022 on the fiftieth anniversary of the federal Clean Water Act of 1972.
2 NEWEA stands for New England Water Environment Association; NEIWPCC stands for the New England Interstate Pollution Control Commission.

Chapter 7

1 Brown, Nell Porter, "Reflections on a River, Paddling the Merrimack in Lowell and Lawrence," Harvard Magazine, July-August 2017.

Chapter 8

1 "Clean Water: Muskie and the Environment," Maine History Online, A Maine Historical Society website," slide exhibit with text.

Chapter 9

1 "Muskie's Legacy," this presentation by Leon Billings is excerpted from the website of the Edmund S. Muskie Foundation, at muskiefoundation.org.

Chapter 12

1 The coverage of the Neuse River was created by author Dyke Hendrickson and is presented to explain why the Neuse was named "River of the Year," by a national environmental organization. My thought was that those involved in cleaning the Merrimack River might learn from those who were successful with the Neuse.

Chapter 17

1 Chapter 17 uses material from the Wikipedia article titled: "Category: Tributaries of the Merrimack River," which is released under the Creative Commons Attribution-Share-Alike License 3.0.

Bibliography

American Rivers, "About the Merrimack," Unsigned written assessment concerning ecological threats (Washington, D.C., 2016)

Blatt, J., director of the Massachusetts Rivers Alliance, interview (Concord, Mass., 2022)

Brinkley, D., *Silent Spring Revolution: John F. Kennedy, Rachel Carson, Lyndon Johnson, Richard Nixon and the Great Environmental Awakenings* (New York, HarperCollins Publishers, 2022)

Casey, B., *All in One River, Falls Dam to Pamlico Sound, Interviewing the Neuse River*, (Chapel Hill, N.C., Chapel Hill Press, 2003)

Cash, D., executive director of the New England division of the federal Environmental Protection Agency, interview (Boston, Mass. 2023)

Cheney, R., *Maritime History of Merrimac Shipbuilding* (Newburyport, Mass., Newburyport Press, 1964)

Chernow, R., *Alexander Hamilton* (New York, Penguin Books, 2004)

Cole, D. B., *Immigrant City, Lawrence, Mass., 1845–1921* (Chapel Hill, North Carolina, University of North Carolina Press, 2002)

Cowley, C., *A History of Lowell, Massachusetts; Lowell, Mass.* (Jazzybee Verlag, 2017)

Currier, J. J., *History of Newbury, Mass, 1635–1902* (Boston, Damrell & Upham, 1902)

The Daily News, Newburyport, Archives of this newspaper were consulted regularly (2022)

Deck, H., executive director of Sound Rivers, an environmental organization in North Carolina, interview (New Bern, N.C., 2022)

DiZoglio, state Sen. D., interview, methods to improve river (2020)

Eagle-Tribune, North Andover, Mass. Archives of this newspaper were consulted regularly (2022)

Eaton, A., *The Amoskeag Manufacturing Company: A History of Enterprise on the Merrimack River* (Charleston, S.C., Arcadia Publishing Co., 2015)

Graovac, D., former chair of the board of the Merrimack River Watershed Council, interview (2022)

Hendrickson, D., *Nautical Newburyport: A History of Captains, Clipper Ships and the Coast Guard* (Charleston, S.C., The History Press, 2017)

Hendrickson, D., *Merrimack: The Resilient River* (Charleston, S.C., Fonthill Media, 2021)
Hendrickson, D., *Plum Island: A Vulnerable Gem* (Charleston, S.C., Fonthill Media, 2022)
Hogg, P., harbormaster of Newburyport, interview (2022)
Hudon, P., *Lower Merrimack: The Valley and Its Peoples: An Illustrated History* (Sun Valley, Calif., American Historical Press, 2004)
Janson, R., former spokesperson for the Environmental Protection Agency in New England, phone interview. Subject was the value of Sen. George Mitchell to the 1987 Amendments of Clean Water Act (2020)
Krop, S., riverkeeper for the Neuse River in North Carolina, interview (New Bern, N.C., 2022)
Macone, J., outreach historian with Merrimack River Watershed Council, interviews (2022–2023)
Maine Historical Society, Maine Memory Network, "Clean Water: Muskie and the Environment," essay (Portland, 2005)
McNeill, F., chief engineer of Manchester, N.H.'s Environmental Protection Division, where he manages northern New England's largest wastewater utility, interview (2022)
Meader, J. W., *The Merrimack River: Its Sources and Its Tributaries* (Boston, B.B. Russell, 1869)
Merrimack River User Survey, Alliance of Climate and Environmental Stewards (Newburyport, 2022)
Morison, S. E., *The Maritime History of Massachusetts, 1783–1860* (Boston, reprint, Northeastern University Press, 1979)
Mitchell, Sen. G., speaking at the Commemoration of the 30th Anniversary of the Clean Water Act., Committee on Environment and Public Works, U.S. Senate, 107th Congress, Second Session (Washington, D.C., 2002)
Prendergast, J., *Lowell: Images of America* (Charleston, S.C. Arcadia Publishing, 1996)
Roberts, J., *The Connecticut River from the Air* (Guilford, Conn., Globe/Pequot Publishing, 2018)
Samson, G., *Manchester: The Mills and The Immigrant Experience* (Portsmouth, N.H., Arcadia Publishing, 2000)
Society for the Protection of the New Hampshire Forests, *River at Risk*, narrated film about the Merrimack River (2021)
Sparks, D., "The Course of the Merrimack, My Time Among the Voyagers," *Merrimack Valley Magazine* (Methuen, Mass., 2019)
Tarr, Sen. B., Massachusetts state senator and the co-chair of the Merrimack River Beach Alliance, interview (2023)
Thoreau, H. D., "A Week on the Concord and Merrimack Rivers, 1849," various reprinted editions.
Wikipedia, "Tributaries of the Merrimack River," en.wikipedia.org/wiki/Merrimack_River

About the Author

Dyke Hendrickson is an author-journalist living in Newburyport, Mass., birthplace of the U.S. Coast Guard. This is his eighth book. Other recent titles include *Plum Island: A Vulnerable Gem* (2022), *Merrimack: The Resilient River* (2021), *New England Coast Guard Stories* (2020), and *Nautical Newburyport* (2017).

The author is a graduate of Franklin and Marshall College with a degree in history, and he did master's work at the University of Maine, Orono. He has been a writer and/or editor with the *Portland Press Herald*, the *New Orleans Times-Picayune*, and the *Boston Herald*. Other publications he has written for include *USA Today*, the *Boston Globe*, and *Tennis* magazine. Most recently, he was the waterfront reporter for *The Daily News* in Newburyport. For several years, he hosted a podcast, *Life Along the Merrimack*, which aired on local cable TV. Hendrickson is a former adjunct professor of journalism at Northeastern University.